# THE
# BAPTISMAL
# LIFE

## REV. DR. MICHAEL BERG

D0584613

**NORTHWESTERN PUBLISHING HOUSE**
Milwaukee, Wisconsin

Northwestern Publishing House
N16W23379 Stone Ridge Dr., Waukesha, WI 53188
www.nph.net
© 2022 Northwestern Publishing House
Published 2022
Printed in the United States of America
ISBN 978-0-8100-3192-0
ISBN 978-0-8100-3193-7 (e-book)

22 23 24 25 26 27 28 29 30 31    10  9  8  7  6  5  4  3  2  1

# CONTENTS

# FOREWORD

The congregation sings in a quiet, darkened sanctuary on that Friday we dare to call "Good":

> O Jesus blest, my help and rest,
> regard my prayerful weeping:
> usher me through death and grave
> safe into your keeping. (CW 427:6)

There is really no room for excuses nor any skillful skirting around the issue at hand at this service. God's own Son is dead, and my faith in humanity is once again dashed to pieces. Even more, the honest confession of those who gather that evening must quietly be said: "I have done this. Lord, have mercy."

The congregation members join together again in a few short days, and one might wonder if they are even in the same place. The sights and smells of the sanctuary have been transformed; instruments and voices strike a new chord, a new song. What of sin? What of death? What of grave and hell? Christ is risen, he's risen indeed, alleluia and amen! Pay attention to this—the Risen One, the firstfruits of those who have fallen asleep—he lives no more to die (1 Corinthians 15).

What should you make of this—this death and resurrection? It is certain, and it is yours. You live no more to die. To borrow from Saint Paul as he writes to the Colossian Christians and the church in Rome: this is neither your first Good Friday nor your first Easter, not for the baptized. In your blessed baptismal waters, you have been put to death and raised to life with Christ.

Now the fun starts. The nurse working feverishly in the baby wing of the local hospital barely lifted her eyes as I made my way past her desk. Did she not know the time had come for a death and resurrection—right in the midst of her 12-hour shift? And those passersby on a Sunday morning—if they steal a glance through the church windows as they cruise by at 40 miles per hour—do they not see the miracle every time it happens? I suppose you cannot blame either the nurse or the passerby, for it all looks so mundane and ordinary that it *seems* as if nothing is happening. This is God's way. In the hands of a feeble man, with the cross marking head and heart, "One redeemed by Christ the crucified." A name is spoken and *the name* is spoken and water is applied. What joys are ours! Adoption, forgiveness, redemption, new life, death, and resurrection.

The church throughout the ages—in poetry and art, in prayers and hymns, in sermons and books—has drawn connections, has told and retold this death and resurrection story. Pastor Berg has done the church of our age (and, I pray, for the next generation too) a great service in this book. In the pages that follow, he connects the dots, traces the story, and connects the great story of salvation with your story.

I refer to the author as Pastor Berg for a reason. While I have been blessed to call the author a classmate and friend and brother in ministry; and have seen him carry out his vocations of son and brother, husband and father; and have witnessed his gifts put to work as Reverend

Doctor and Professor; this book is no mere treatise for academia's sake. Rather, it flows from Mike's work as pastor, a true shepherd of those entrusted to his care, one who dared to stand up and speak for the once was dead but now quite alive Christ Jesus. That sermon, preached to a group not at all unlike you, dear reader, is expanded here for those who are baptized and, I pray, for those who are not, for those who might be wondering and asking.

There are many ways to tell one's story, and by virtue of your baptism, yours is quite a marvelous story to tell:

- What of your Father? His name for you: "Beloved"!
- What of your sin? It has been washed away.
- What of your name? A new name has been given. You are now his.
- What of your inheritance? Signed, sealed, and delivered.
- What of your struggles? You know who goes with you: he who knows your struggles. He has lived them.
- What of your ability to forgive? Truly, all things are possible through him who gives you strength.
- What of your hope? It is certain.
- What of your expectations for the new day and the confidence to lay your head on your pillow at night? "In the name of the Father and of the Son and of the Holy Spirit"—you know who you wake with and in whose name you go back to sleep.
- What of your death? You have already died. What is there to fear?
- What of your life? That which is yours forever allows you to live today as well.

Dead in Christ. Alive in Christ. What about this life of yours? The last few years have brought a few "old but new to us" traditions to accompany my family's Easter celebrations. New shoes remind the household that as God's Easter children, the baptized, we get to walk about in newness of life. Freshly washed eyes in the morning remind the household that as God's Easter children, the baptized, we get to see life in a new way. The old has gone, the new has come. Baptism means laughter and love, mercy and forgiveness, a listening ear and a warm witness. Baptism means all that is his is yours. And I'll be bold to ask: is there any other life worth living?

Back to the sanctuary. There stands the font. How many have died and risen there? The paschal candle is lit, the mystery of Good Friday and Easter, your own Good Friday and Easter, brightly shining—not even death is able to snuff out the love of Christ. Front and center, at the base of the chancel steps, lies your body, possibly draped with a funeral pall, a symbol of the righteousness freely given in Christ. There you are, you dead and alive one. What shall they sing as it looks, oh, so final?

> Death, you cannot end my gladness:
> I am baptized into Christ!
> When I die, I leave all sadness
> to inherit paradise!
> Though I lie in dust and ashes
> faith's assurance brightly flashes:
> Baptism has the strength divine
> to make life immortal mine.

There is nothing worth comparing
to this lifelong comfort sure!
Open-eyed my grave is staring:
even there I'll sleep secure.
Though my flesh awaits its raising,
still my soul continues praising:
I am baptized into Christ;
I'm a child of paradise! (CW 679:4,5)

John Bortulin
Eastertide 2022

# INTRODUCTION

If you pay attention, you will notice that God's Word is dripping wet. Everywhere you turn, there seems to be water. Story after story uses water imagery. Sometimes the water is as mysterious as it was in the beginning when the Spirit hovered over the deep. Sometimes it is destructive like in the flood in Noah's day. Sometimes it is delightful like the river that flows in Ezekiel's vision, gently watering the land. Each image points directly or indirectly to—or at least reminds us of—a washing away of sins and redemption in Christ, the whole point of the Bible. God's Word is dripping wet. So is your everyday life. Water is everywhere you look. Water is fundamental to creation and preserves life. You cannot survive without it. But here is the thing about water: It is both good and bad. We need water, but water can devastate. Water both destroys and saves. Water humbles and exalts. Spiritually, water both kills and resurrects. This watery image we trace through Scripture is all part of the story of salvation. It is a story of cleansing. It is a story of sins washed away. It is the story of death and resurrection. It is a story of Baptism. As a Christian, it is your story.

This red line starts with a watery creation and ends with the river of the water of life flowing from the throne of the Lamb. Eden's rivers gently watered the garden. But we don't travel very far through the pages of Scripture until we find water violently flooding the world. Water marked the beginning of freedom from slavery and the crossing over to the Promised Land. We are told that Israel was baptized into Moses. Those same Israelites were marked with circumcision, a blessing from Aaron the priest, and oil (all three are related to Baptism). They were baptized (washed) with ceremonial washings that taught them about sin and grace until Christ came and truly baptized with a washing away of sin. We keep going and see that Naaman was washed in the Jordan River. John baptized there too. Christ himself entered the baptismal waters of the same river. Ezekiel and John alike saw a vision of fresh water renewing this earth into a new and everlasting Eden. Water, water everywhere.

As with many pictures, this water imagery finds its fulfillment in the New Testament, specifically in Jesus Christ. The images may start off vague, but they become clear at the cross. All things point to Calvary. The red line culminates at the crucifixion, not in crystal clear water but in red blood. Yet it does not end there. After this red line runs through the pages of Holy Scripture, it jumps up and out of the Bible and into the hands of a pastor as he says these words: "I baptize you." At your baptism the story of Scripture became your story from beginning to end. You were made a part of the story, even the main focus of the story. The baptized are connected to Christ in a most intimate way: They die and rise with him. This is not simply a onetime event even though Baptism only occurs once in the life of a Christian. It is a life of dying and living. It is a life of cross and resurrection. And in the end, when all is done and life is in the rearview mirror, you will realize that this Christian life of yours was dripping wet. It was, in fact, a baptismal life from beginning to end.

This book will trace the water story from Genesis to Revelation in a chiastic form. The first chapter relates to the last chapter. The second chapter relates to the second to last chapter, culminating in the middle with, who else, Christ and his death and resurrection. He pulls you into his death and resurrection via Baptism and makes your life a baptismal life.

## 2.

# A WATERY CREATION

The dawn of time. No elements, no form, only God. A Creator without a creation. A blank canvas. The artist begins. It is only out of his imagination that anything we know as real came about. It could have been a creation without the concept of time. It could have been a creation that did not rely on oxygen, a creation that had no atmosphere. It could have been a creation with no gravity. The possibilities were endless because there were no boundaries. It could have been a creation without water. But the imagination of God gave us a world "formed out of water and by water" (2 Peter 3:5).

All three persons of the Trinity were present at this watery creation. The church father Irenaeus once said that God made humankind with his two hands, the Son and the Holy Spirit.[1] John the evangelist—who, by the way, taught Ignatius, who taught Polycarp, who taught Irenaeus—is a little more precise: "Through him all things were made; without him nothing was made that has been made" (John 1:3). Christ was not only there at the creation; all things were created through him. He

---

[1]Alexander Roberts and James Donaldson, eds., *The Ante-Nicean Fathers,* Vol. 1 (Peabody, Massachusetts: Hendrikson Publishers, 1994), p. 463.

really is the beginning and the end, the Alpha and Omega (Revelation 22:13).

Yet there is more. John labeled Jesus Christ "the Word." "In the beginning was the Word, and the Word was with God, and the Word was God" (John 1:1). The Greek word translated as "the Word" is *logos*. Logos is an interesting word. This is where we get all the "ologies." If you want to study the order of life (*bio*), then you will study *biology*. If you want to study God (*theo*), then you study *theology*. *Logos* can mean "order," "word," even "reason" or "calculation." God spoke in the beginning and order was created. The eternal Logos is the reason up is up and down is down. He is the reason that 2 plus 2 equals 4 and not 7. He is the Alpha and Omega, the beginning and the end, and everything in between! He is the Word. He is the Logos.

Then there is the Spirit. He hovered over the deep. The Hebrew verb we read as "hover" brings to mind the fluttering of a bird. Perhaps a hint of how the Holy Spirit will appear later in Scripture, particularly at another water event: the baptism of Jesus. So we have this mysterious water, the Spirit hovering, and the eternal Word all at this wonderful creation. All three persons of the Trinity were present—and there was water too.

God then split and gathered the waters (Genesis 1:6-9). He did this with his words. "God said, 'Let there be a vault between the waters to separate water from water.' So God made the vault and separated the water under the vault from the water above it. And it was so" (Genesis 1:6,7). "God said, 'Let the water under the sky be gathered to one place, and let dry ground appear.' And it was so" (Genesis 1:9). When God speaks, things happen.

Words have power; God's words have creative power. Things are created from nothing. When God said, "Let there be light," there was light.

Both water and words, while different, are fundamental to this world. They both have power seemingly beyond their nature. They seem so small, but they both destroy and sustain. Water can do great damage, as anybody living in a floodplain will attest—or anybody with a basement for that matter. Yet water is essential to our existence. Most of the earth is water. We might say that we have a love-hate relationship with water. It quenches thirst and cools us at the beach or by a pool. A hot shower revitalizes us. A cleansing afternoon rain refreshes the earth. But a simple leak can cause expensive damage. Floods can wash away property and people. A tsunami can engulf whole cities. Water gives life, refreshes, and revitalizes, but brings death and damage too.

Likewise, words destroy and build. We might think of the joy of a conversation with an old friend or the grandiose words of a constitution. We might think about literature that soars or poetry that moves. Yet words can destroy. Hurtful words cut deeper than any knife, and political rhetoric can instigate violence and hate. Words are as fundamental to our human existence as water is. We were created by words. We interact with fellow human beings primarily through words. We interact with God with words. We are to take God at his word. From the very beginning there was water and words: water, words, and Spirit.

There is another event in which the Father, Son, and Spirit used water and Word to create something out of nothing. Actually, there are many events in which the

Holy Trinity works this creative miracle: baptisms. God's Word can create a living faith in a dead heart. Paul connects these two creative acts of God: "God, who said, 'Let light shine out of darkness,' made his light shine in our hearts to give us the light of the knowledge of God's glory displayed in the face of Christ" (2 Corinthians 4:6). The sinful nature is dead. It cannot spring to life in faith. It needs a miracle. It needs a rebirth. It needs God's creative Word. At Baptism, a living faith is created in a dead heart with water and Word. This is no less a miracle and no less important than when God said, "Let there be light." Baptism is a creative act. "If anyone is in Christ, he is a new creation; the old has gone, the new has come!" (2 Corinthians 5:17 NIV 1984). God says, "Let there be a believing heart," and there is.

# 3.

# THE RIVER OF EDEN

We are told that the beautiful garden in Eden was naturally watered by rivers. Even before God planted the Garden of Eden, he made sure that his whole creation was watered. "Now no shrub had yet appeared on the earth and no plant had yet sprung up, for the Lord God had not sent rain on the earth and there was no one to work the ground, but streams came up from the earth and watered the whole surface of the ground" (Genesis 2:5,6). Later, after creating humans and planting the garden in Eden for them to work, God put a "river watering the garden" that "flowed from Eden; from there it was separated into four headwaters" (Genesis 2:10).

God took care of his creation and, specifically, he took care of Adam and Eve. Fresh springs did the work of irrigation. Perhaps we don't understand how uncertain water access truly is. We turn on a faucet and expect water to flow. We demand it. It is our right. We are incensed at the local municipality when the water pressure is low. But if you pay attention to local (and global) politics, you know that the right to water is one of the most contested issues. Access to a fresh stream or spring is vital to the survival of a community, but it is far from guaranteed. Once again we see the importance and power of water. Once again we see the care God displays for his new creation.

his. We are a part of his church and are coworkers with him in the world. Christians are given a divine purpose in everyday life. God calls us to love our neighbors. We are God's masks. God puts us on as if we were his mask. We become God's coworkers in the world. God feeds the world through farmers and grocers. He teaches our children through educators and heals through doctors and nurses. Christ provides not only for our physical needs and our eternal needs, but he hands us also a reason to live. He gives us a job, many jobs in fact. Don't underestimate your need to work, have purpose, and be productive. We innately know that we are not satisfied with eighty to one hundred years with death looming. Nor we will be satisfied with subsistence living. We know that we, created in the image of God, are important and valuable. We are thirsty, and Christ quenches that thirst. He makes us his.

He made us his with another water event: Baptism. The living water of Christ who is the Water of Life is also the baptizer. He provides his Word that ends all thirst, but he also washes with water. Both God's Word and remembrances of our baptisms refresh us along our sometimes bitter journey in this life. Our eyes are lifted up to see more than an oasis in this wilderness journey: we see the end. We see paradise, a paradise given to us through the adoption of Baptism. The bitter waters we encounter in our life are actually good for us. They push us to look up for something better. They move us to yearn for paradise. They also connect us to Christ (1 Peter 4:13). We are his coworkers. Should we not suffer as he did? Should we need to suffer with him? In the end, those bitter waters (suffering) are made fresh in Christ. We are secure both in our final destination and our wilderness journey.

4.

# THE FLOOD

God had created man in his own image. A perfect image. Adam and Eve had no shame. They were comfortable in their bodies. They didn't mind being naked. Things ran smoothly. It was the one and only perfect marriage. Things changed, though. Adam and Eve were created with the ability not to sin. But they did. Sin slithered its way into the world, forever changing God's perfect creation. Sin multiplied quickly. It didn't take long for the first homicide to occur: it took only one generation for Cain to take Abel's life. His own brother no less. The first homicide was the first fratricide. Things spiraled out of control. It got bad, really bad.

This is how Moses described the state of affairs before God commanded Noah to build the ark: "The LORD saw how great man's wickedness on the earth had become, and that every inclination of the thoughts of his heart was only evil all the time. The LORD regretted that he had made human beings on the earth, and his heart was filled with pain" (Genesis 6:5,6 NIV 1984). Notice the piling up of terms: *every, only, all the time.* No wonder God grieved. The artist's creation was ruined.

Our grieving God decided to destroy what he made, but not all of it. He would wipe humankind from the earth, but not everyone. He had made a promise. A promise with words. It was a *promise-Word*. God gave his word and he always keeps his word. He would save humankind from the sinful condition they made for themselves. He would do both with water. He would destroy and save with water—the very same water.

This was terrifying. Many of us grew up with a sanitized version of many biblical stories. None more so than this horrific flood. Perhaps in your nursery there was a painting of Noah's ark that resembled a floating zoo instead of a crowded floating cage with animals jammed into rooms. How cute are those giraffes with heads sticking out of a window?! You learned the names of these animals, the lions, zebras, and camels. They seemed so happy. We forget the horror of the seas rising and desperate people fighting for the highest ground, the last bit of real estate before being washed away. Mothers holding their children high above their heads before the inevitable death at sea. The ancients felt this. The sea was a mysterious and dangerous place. It is hard for us who are used to cruise ships and planes that travel safely above the chaos. The depths did not beckon human exploration but, rather, produced nightmarish tales.

Perhaps we do the same with Baptism. It's cute. A child in a white gown. Smiling parents. Proud grandparents capturing the sweet scene with a camera. There will be a party, a cake, and presents. But the truth is that this gentle bath is also a drowning. It is a violent scene. The devil contends for this precious soul. A battle wages. God versus Satan. Sin versus grace. Heaven versus hell. Death versus life. Think of Martin Luther's answer to his own question in the Small Catechism: "What does baptizing with water mean? Baptism means that the old Adam in us should be drowned by daily contrition and repentance, and that all its evil deeds and desires be put to death. It also means that a new person should daily arise to live before God in righteousness and purity forever."[2]

Luther's catechetical instruction is nothing more than an application of Paul's words to the Romans, "Don't you know that all of us who were baptized into Christ Jesus were baptized into his death? We were therefore buried with him through baptism into death in order that, just as Christ was raised from the dead through the glory of the Father, we too may live a new life" (Romans 6:3,4). Baptism is a death and resurrection. It is a drowning but also a crucifixion. There are not many more violent ways to die. Baptism is just as violent as the flood if we see it through the lens of the cross.

Why is it such a violent scene? Because a human is valuable, that's why. Don't you understand how valuable you are to both God and the devil? Think of the monumental effort that has been exerted on both sides of the battlefield fighting over you. God became man for you. This is arguably the greatest miracle of all: the infinite one becomes the finite one. He lived a difficult life for you. He willingly suffered at the hands of men, was crucified, and was buried. He then performed another astonishing miracle by rising from the dead. He sent the Holy Spirit to you. He ascended into heaven to prepare a place in heaven for you. He rules all things for your benefit and plans on returning for you. Not to mention his constant protection, care, and love. He sent you parents

---

[2]*Luther's Catechism* (Milwaukee: Northwestern Publishing House, 2017), p. 10.

and teachers, friends and family, a pastor to preach to you, and a congregation to huddle around you. And then there is all we do not see, such as guardian angels. This is how valuable you are to God.

God is willing to wage a cosmic battle for your future. For all that God does for you, seen and unseen, the devil too is working hard for your soul. Think of all the tricks he uses and all the temptations he sends. He tempts you with excess and self-pity. He urges you to believe in yourself and not your God. He wants you to believe that you control your own destiny, that you belong wholly to yourself and not to him. Satan's greatest trick, perhaps, is to even convince you that he does not exist and therefore is not a threat. This is how valuable you are to him. He is willing to obscure his own identity and even existence so that you believe there is no real danger because no danger means no need of a Savior.

So God needs to fight for you. It is a violent battle. So violent that it ends in a crucifixion and resurrection. A violent death and a violent breaking of a deathly tomb. If you could see the unseen, you would see angels and demons, perhaps standing on either side of you. We are people between God and the devil. It is that serious. But we are also secure: Don't you know that all of you who are baptized have already been through the battle with Christ? You have already died. You have already been buried. You have already been resurrected. It is a fact of history. It is that secure.

These violent scenes are rightly depicted with joy. The flood ends with a rainbow—another prom-ise attached to a physical element. The light reflects through the moist air and words are spoken. Never again! Never again would such a terror be visited upon God's creation—he promised. The dove sent by Noah retrieves an olive branch. Peace. Another fluttering over water, but this time with the water receding to its proper place. The very same water that destroyed also pushed the ark high above the chaos and saved Noah and his family, eight in all. The world was handed back to Noah and all his descendants as a gift to be enjoyed once again. All will be well in the end.

So we should eat our cake and throw a party too. The parents should smile and the grandparents should be proud. The battle has been won. The waters recede back into the font, having fallen through the pastor's fingers or gently over a silver shell or, perhaps more symbolically, off the child who was immersed in the flood of Baptism and resurrected from this watery grave as a redeemed child of God. All will be well in the end. And the Spirit hovers even if we cannot see him. The very same water that drowns the sinful nature in Baptism saves a Christian from sin.

But why Noah? Was he so special? Yes and no. We are told that God grieved over the sinfulness of humankind but that "Noah found favor in the eyes of the LORD" and that "Noah was a righteous man" (Genesis 6:8,9). Noah first was given the favor of God. He found acceptance with God; that is, God accepted him in grace. Noah was a sinner. He made that obviously clear after the flood (Genesis 9:21). So how can he be called righteous? It is because Jesus was righteous in his place. The patriarchs of the Old Testament trusted in God and their faith was credited to them as righteousness (Genesis 15:6; Romans 3:21-24). It certainly took faith to build this large boat. So

We understand that advertisers want to sell us a product or experience. We know they are manipulating us with song, story, and picture. We accept it and adjust. We don't really believe that a car purchase will make our lives completely different. We know that politicians stump for votes and that the truth is hidden under all the rhetoric. We accept it and recalibrate. We know that companies, employers, neighbors, acquaintances, and even our friends will bend the truth. Not so for the ancients. Sure, they were as much liars as we are, but there was something about taking vows back then. A person's word mattered. Even the evil Herod kept his word when Herodias asked for John the Baptist's head (Matthew 14:1,2). He knew that it wasn't wise to behead John, but what could he do? He made a promise.

This certainly doesn't mean that the ancient Near East was a pious place. On the contrary, it was a violent place. All you have to do is read the book of Judges or any other ancient text to cringe at the violence and debauchery. We look back with moral disgust at this time seemingly devoid of human rights, but we should catch ourselves. We have modern faults about which the ancients would be rightly appalled. They may have been quick to take up arms, but they kept their word. Or at least they took vows with more seriousness than we do. Could it be a remnant of God's powerful creation through words? Words mattered.

God gave his word to Abram. He would have a family and a land, and from that family and land, a Savior. God marked this promise with a surgery. A particular part of skin from a particular part of the male body would be removed. The family of Abram and, indeed, the whole of Israel would be marked. They were different. They had a different purpose. They were to bring about the Savior of the world. From *their* flesh. No wonder it was that part of the body. Every male would be reminded of his purpose, God's Word, and God's salvation multiple times a day. It was a gritty world back then!

Circumcision identified Israel as the bearers of the seed of the promise. It also identified the Israelites as free people. There were many times in Israel's history when we call them anything but free: in Egypt, under the thumb of the Philistines, in exile in Babylon, even under Roman rule in the New Testament era. The soldiers who entered the Promised Land behind the general, Joshua, were circumcised before the battle at Jericho. We are told that God "rolled away the reproach of Egypt" (Joshua 5:9) and that the manna stopped and they ate from their own land. They weren't slaves anymore; they were free people. In fact, the Israelites always maintained that they were free people; that is, they were the ones created in the image of God, loved by God, and made free by God. When Jesus told a crowd that he would set them free, they protested, "We are Abraham's descendants and have never been slaves of anyone. How can you say that we shall be set free?" (John 8:33). What the crowd did not understand was that Jesus would truly set them free—free from sin and death. Their circumcised identity was only a shadow of a baptized identity. A free people identity.

Back to Abraham. God took a vow the day he made a covenant with Abram. He promised to bring about a son for Abram and a Son for the world. Abram, in turn, promised to perform this surgery as a sign of God's vow. Abram too made a vow. But human promises stink.

Even the promises of those ancient people, who took vows far more seriously than us, were suspect. This was finally about God's promise, God's vow, and God's promise-Word. This was about God marking his people. Abram, now Abraham, would be the father not only of the nation later known as Israel, but also the spiritual father of all believers everywhere, regardless of ethnicity, class, or gender, even regardless of circumcision. For the spiritual Israel there would be more than a circumcision of the body; there would be a circumcision of the heart.

After Christ was born, the law of circumcision was no longer in effect. It had served its purpose. The law was to separate Israel from other nations. This did not mean that only Israelites were loved by God. On the contrary, there were believers in God outside of the physical and ethnic boundaries of Israel. The point was to keep Israel intact for the specific purpose of bringing about the Messiah. This is Israel's glory: It would be the priesthood to the world. Its prophets would speak truth to the nations. Its Messiah would be everybody's Messiah. The law of circumcision marked these men of Israel, and indeed the whole nation, as the caretakers of this promise. The Messiah would come from them.

Circumcision has been called an Old Testament sacrament. God made a promise, and his promise-Word was attached to a physical symbol. Yet this was nothing without faith. Consider Saint Paul's words to the Roman congregation:

> Is this blessedness only for the circumcised, or also for the uncircumcised? We have been say-ing that Abraham's faith was credited to him as

righteousness. Under what circumstances was it credited? Was it after he was circumcised, or before? It was not after, but before! And he received circumcision as a sign, a seal of the righteousness that he had by faith while he was still uncircumcised. So then, he is the father of all who believe but have not been circumcised, in order that righteousness might be credited to them. And he is then also the father of the circumcised who not only are circumcised but who also follow in the footsteps of the faith that our father Abraham had before he was circumcised. (Romans 4:9-12)

Circumcision was not about following a law, as if God was somehow pleased with the empty ritual of this surgery (Romans 2:25-29). It was about God's promise and the faith that results. For Abraham it was a faith in the future Messiah. This was about God's action, not man's action.

Baptism is the New Testament counterpart of circumcision. Like all New Testament realities of Old Testament shadows, Baptism is the real deal. Baptism is not a symbol of a future reality as was circumcision. Baptism delivers grace. It is a sacrament in the New Testament sense. God attached his promise-Word to this physical water. This physical promise-Word delivers grace. Read Saint Paul again:

In Christ all the fullness of the Deity lives in bodily form, and in Christ you have been brought to fullness. He is the head over every power and authority. In him you were also circumcised with a circumcision not performed by human hands. Your whole self ruled by the flesh was put off when you were circumcised by Christ, having been buried with him in baptism, in which you were also raised with him through your faith in the working of God, who raised him from the dead. When you were dead in your sins and in the uncircumcision of your flesh, God made you alive with Christ. He forgave us all our sins, having canceled the charge of our legal indebtedness, which stood against us and condemned us; he has taken it away, nailing it to the cross. (Colossians 2:9-14)

God's saving work in Baptism is nothing else than Christ taking away sins. It is a circumcision of the heart. Sin is cut away. It is spiritual surgery. The sinful nature dies and the new creation arises. This careful surgery is the application of law and gospel. The law cuts. Really, it kills. Like a hammer it shatters us to pieces by dramatically pointing out our depravity. We have no hope in ourselves. The gospel, on the other hand, makes alive. The circumcised men of ancient Israel believed and it was credited to them as righteousness (Genesis 15:6). Their faith was in the One to come. On the other side of the Messiah's passion, baptized Christians believe in what has been done to them. They are crucified with Christ and have been resurrected with him (Romans 6:1-3). They have a circumcision of the heart.

## 6.

# A WATER EXODUS

Four hundred years is a long time. A long time to be away from home. A long time to be someone else's labor. The Israelites were far from their home for a long time, but they did have reminders of the Promised Land. Surely this helped keep their hopes alive. The truth was passed down from generation to generation. They had entered Egypt as a family but left as a nation. They survived the great famine in Joseph's day and were spared starvation because Joseph taxed the Egyptians during the seven years of abundance that proceeded the seven years of famine. The grain that Pharaoh collected spared both Egypt and Israel during the famine. But when Joseph lay in his tomb in the midst of his Hebrew people, Pharaoh turned against the growing nation. He enslaved them. Years later they would even face an infanticide to keep their numbers—and the threat to Egypt—low.

For the most part, the Israelites kept themselves separate from the Egyptians, not only because of their social standing but also because of their culture. They had a visual reminder too. The embalmed body of Joseph was laid among the people of Israel. His bones were to be buried in the Promised Land whenever God finally led his people there. And just as it took an act of God to preserve Noah and his family, so it would take an act of God

see today you will never see again. The LORD will fight for you; you need only to be still." (Exodus 14:10-14)

The Israelites had nowhere to turn but God. All they were to do was to be still and let God be God. All they needed to do was watch God use water again. Saint Paul connects this water event with another water event, Baptism:

I do not want you to be ignorant of the fact, brothers and sisters, that our ancestors were all under the cloud and that they all passed through the sea. They were all baptized into Moses in the cloud and in the sea. They all ate the same spiritual food and drank the same spiritual drink; for they drank from the spiritual rock that accompanied them, and that rock was Christ. (1 Corinthians 10:1-4)

God was with them with a pillar of cloud by day and a pillar of fire by night. He split the Red Sea for the sake of their freedom. Notice the vague but powerful imagery of both water (cloud and Red Sea) and fire. It was a baptism of water and of fire (see Luke 3:16). How? The Israelites were connected intimately with their leader, Moses, and therefore to their protector, God. They were given freedom from slavery. Their enemy was defeated. They emerged for a new life. They would be protected. They were baptized into Moses. They had God's protection.

Those baptized into Christ have a leader and an enemy too. They also are trapped. They have nowhere to go. Who will save them from death? Who will free them from the slavery to sin? Can a doctor stop death? Can a government truly give absolute freedom? Moses' wooden staff split the Red Sea, but Christ's wooden cross saves. The cross makes Baptism a saving act resulting in freedom as the enemy's charioteers rapidly draw near. Christians are baptized not into Moses but into Christ. They have God's eternal protection.

The freedom of Israel was not free. Freedom is never free, and the going price for freedom is almost always blood. The freedom of Israel cost blood and not just any blood but firstborn blood. The son of Pharaoh and many others died. God never let the Israelites forget this. Even before they escaped through the Red Sea, he instituted a meal of remembrance. The Passover meal recounted the exodus for countless generations. The Israelites in Egypt were to eat a special meal: a meal of lamb and unleavened bread. The blood of those lambs was to be smeared on the doorframes of their homes. It marked them as God's people. Blood marked them. The Angel of the Lord would come with the full wrath of the deity to take firstborn blood, both animal and human. But the angel would pass over the bloodstained homes, sparing the firstborn of Israel. The Passover meal was then celebrated every year and, in some cases, every week as a reminder of Israel's escape. They would never forget.

There is another way God reminded the Israelites of their miraculous escape from slavery. It's a little complicated but profound. God commanded that every firstborn male of every Israelite family would be consecrated to him. Here is what God told Moses to say to the Israelites:

"Consecrate to me every firstborn male. The first offspring of every womb among the Israelites belongs to me, whether human or animal.

"After the LORD brings you into the land of the Canaanites and gives it to you, as he promised on oath to you and your ancestors, you are to give over to the LORD the first offspring of every womb. All the firstborn males of your livestock belong to the LORD. Redeem with a lamb every firstborn donkey, but if you do not redeem it, break its neck. Redeem every firstborn among your sons.

"In days to come, when your son asks you, 'What does this mean?' say to him, 'With a mighty hand the LORD brought us out of Egypt, out of the land of slavery. When Pharaoh stubbornly refused to let us go, the LORD killed the firstborn of both people and animals in Egypt. This is why I sacrifice to the LORD the first male offspring of every womb and redeem each of my firstborn sons.' And it will be like a sign on your hand and a symbol on your forehead that the LORD brought us out of Egypt with his mighty hand." (Exodus 13:2,11-16)

It was as if God said, "Freedom isn't free. It costs firstborn blood. You owe me. You owe me firstborn blood. Consecrate your firstborns to me." Israel's freedom was procured by water and blood. Miraculous water and firstborn blood. And they were never to forget.

But God did not desire more bloodshed. Nor does he ever desire empty ritual. Just like circumcision was not about the vow Abram took but, rather, a teaching tool to remind the Israelites of God's vow, so this law of consecration was not really about God demanding payment but to show the people of God that there would be payment made on their behalf. It wasn't empty ritual; it was a foreshadow of things to come, namely, Christ.

Fast-forward to 40 days after Jesus' birth. Mary and Joseph, faithful Jewish parents in first-century Palestine, traveled to the temple to fulfill this ancient command. They entered into the presence of God to present their firstborn boy to the Lord. They came to consecrate him. They would not sacrifice him. Nor would they leave him to work in the temple as Hannah did with Samuel. Rather, they would redeem their infant boy. They would buy him back; that is what the word *redeem* means. The price was blood once again: a lamb or, if they were poor (and they were), two pigeons or doves. So they bought back Jesus with a sacrifice of animals. They were descendants of the tribes of Israel. They were free (sort of) and owed God for their freedom and their Promised Land. And the going price for freedom is almost always blood.

But we cannot escape the irony. It would be their son, the Son of God, who would be the sacrifice that would redeem all of Israel from the slavery of sin and death. He was the payment. It was his blood. It was firstborn blood, not just their firstborn but the firstborn of God (Colossians 1:15). No longer would Jewish families be required to buy back their firstborn. The payment would be made at the cross. All this is a precursor to another trip to Jerusalem:

> "We are going up to Jerusalem," [Jesus] said, "and the Son of Man will be delivered over to the chief priests and the teachers of the law. They will condemn him to death and will hand him over to the Gentiles, who will mock him and spit on him, flog him and kill him. Three days later he will rise. . . . For even the Son of Man did not come to be served, but to serve, and to give his life as a ransom for many." (Mark 10:33,34,45)

There needed to be blood, but it wouldn't be Mary's or Joseph's blood (nor ours); it would be God's own blood. Freedom is never free.

# 7.

# THE WILDERNESS JOURNEY

We talk a lot about freedom, but the truth is that we can't handle freedom. It's too much for us. It is too profound, too glorious, too beyond us sinful creatures. The freed slaves of Israel grumbled and complained so much about their freedom that God barred that generation from the Promised Land. Even before they crossed the Red Sea they said, "Was it because there were no graves in Egypt that you brought us to the desert to die? What have you done to us by bringing us out of Egypt? Didn't we say to you in Egypt, 'Leave us alone; let us serve the Egyptians'? It would have been better for us to serve the Egyptians than to die in the desert!" (Exodus 14:11,12).

Freedom is hard. The security of the law seems so attractive to us. It seems comforting and easy: No responsibility. No worries. Someone else will take care of it for us. All we have to do is give up some privileges. The history of humankind is awash with the tension between freedom and security. So it was for the Israelites. At least in Egypt they had three square meals a day. They even began to detest God's heavenly bread and quail as "miserable food" (Numbers 21:5).

True freedom is not freedom from suffering (at least not on earth); true freedom is love. If we are sinners (and we are), then we are slaves to sin. We cannot stop sinning. We are addicts, as it were. If you doubt this, then why haven't you stopped sinning already? It's not like sin has ever benefited humankind. So "freedom" to do what we want, especially without consequences, is not freedom but slavery to the addiction of sin. We are slaves to sin (Romans 6:20). But the redeemed in Christ are not only sinners but simultaneously saints (holy). A sinner cannot do anything but sin, but a saint cannot do anything but holy deeds. A saint is a slave to righteousness (Romans 6:22). You are free to be whom God has made you to be: righteous. Freedom is love.

Once again there is an identity crisis. Who were the Israelites? Slaves or free people? Spiritually, they were both. They were slaves to sin, craving the law, even slavery. Why? Because sinners cannot trust God. Sinners are unbelievers. Sinners trust themselves and not God to make themselves righteousness. They are stuck in righteousness by law (Romans 3). But those who believed were also saints. They trusted. They believed and it was credited to them as righteousness. They were righteous by faith (Romans 3:21-23). They were free people.

So it is with every believer. Who are we: free or enslaved? On this side of heaven, the answer is yes. We are both. But there is a promised land made for free people. Before Christians enter into this heavenly promised land, there is a time of trial and tribulation we endure as sinner-saints. The ancient Israelites wandered in the wilderness for 40 years. We "wander" in the wilderness of this world, longing for our heavenly home.

The number 40 is all over the Bible. There are too many occurrences to recount. Here are a few: It rained for 40 days and nights as the world was flooded. Moses remained on Mount Sinai for 40 days, and Elijah fasted for 40 days. The number also makes an appearance in the New Testament. Like Elijah, Jesus fasted for 40 days and nights. He did this in the wilderness beyond the Jordan River, where he was tempted by the devil with three distinct temptations. He was tempted to turn stone into bread. He was tempted to bow down to the devil in exchange for power over the kingdoms of the world. Finally, he was tempted with jumping from the pinnacle of the temple and having angels catch him. In each temptation the devil tried to lure the perfect Son of God into sin. He even used Scripture to tempt Jesus. This showdown had eternal ramifications for you and me. If Jesus failed, then he was not righteous. And if he was not righteous, then we cannot be made righteous. Then all would be lost. We would be left to be judged by our own records, and that is not good for sinners.

Jesus combated twisted Scripture with true Scripture. He took the Father at his word. When the starving Jesus was told by the devil to feed himself, Jesus responded with Deuteronomy 8:3: "Man does not live on bread alone but on every word that comes from the mouth of the LORD." When tempted with all the kingdoms of the world, Jesus fought back with another passage from Deuteronomy (6:13): "Worship the Lord your God, and serve him only" (Matthew 4:10). When the devil tried to coax Jesus to plunge from the temple, Jesus retorted, "Do not put the Lord your God to the test" (Matthew 4:7).

That last command quoted by Jesus also came from Deuteronomy chapter 6. The full version reads: "Do not put the LORD your God to the test as you did at Massah" (Deuteronomy 6:16). The Israelites were given these commands, but they failed. They camped at Rephidim but continued to complain to Moses, "Why did you bring us up out of Egypt to make us and our children and live-stock die of thirst?" (Exodus 17:3). Moses, in turn, complained to God, "What am I to do with these people? They are almost ready to stone me" (Exodus 17:4). The Lord instructed Moses to take his staff, the one he lifted over the waters to split the Red Sea, and strike the rock at Horeb to bring forth water for his people. The place was called Massah and Meribah because it was the place of testing (Massah) and quarreling (Meribah).

Notice that Jesus goes out from the Promised Land into the wilderness, the same wilderness in which the Israelites traveled and eventually crossed into Canaan. Notice also that the Israelites were tempted with testing God (at Massah, which means "testing"), with food (they needed to rely on God for manna, of which they complained), and with power (they wanted to control their own destiny and become like the strong military powers around them or, in their more desperate moment, to go back to the "protection" of the pharaoh). Notice that Jesus does what Israel could not do. He stood up under temptation. He is the perfect Israel. He too was called out of Egypt (Matthew 2:19). He too spent time in the wilderness (40 days instead of 40 years). He too was tempted in the wilderness. The difference is that he did not fall into temptation. He did it all for us. His righteousness becomes our righteousness.

So Israel's journey, as we will see, is bookended with water: the Red Sea at the beginning of their 40-year journey and the Jordan River at the end. It was a 40-year journey that was only successful because of God's righteous faithfulness to his promise-Word and decid-edly not because of the actions of Israel. So it is with our Christian journey, our baptismal life. We begin with water and end with the same promise as we enter into our promised land. It is a journey of trial and temptation. It's a number 40 kind of life. Are we not tempted with the material, with power, with testing God? But Jesus succeeds where we fail. He is our righteousness.

Jesus did not strike the rock with anger as Moses did, but rather he absorbed the blows of his own people at the cross. Oh, and one more thing. It is not a coincidence that Jesus spent 40 days after his resurrection showing himself to his followers. After the resurrection and before his ascension (40 days), he proved that he was alive to them so they would have hope in their "40-year" journey to the heavenly promised land. He even redeems the number 40 for us!

## 8.

# BLESSING AND OIL

God marked the Israelites with circumcision, but he also marked them with words. We might even say that he tattooed them with words:

> The LORD said to Moses, "Tell Aaron and his sons, 'This is how you are to bless the Israelites. Say to them: "The LORD bless you and keep you; the LORD make his face shine on you and be gracious to you; the LORD turn his face toward you and give you peace." ' So they will put my name on the Israelites, and I will bless them." (Numbers 6:22-27)

Once again we see that words matter. Words have power. God's words have power. These words are not empty but backed up by the God of power. His words are active. They are sent out to accomplish what he desires and do not return to him empty-handed (Isaiah 55:11).

This Aaronic blessing "put" God's name in the Israelites. They were branded once again. This time not with surgery of flesh but with promise-Word, an invisible brand, or tattoo, that marked the Israelites as belonging to God. They were *his* people. They belonged to him. This is more than belonging to a gang or a military regiment or a close-knit group of friends (all relationships in which a tattoo might signify belonging). This is an ownership. Branding an animal signifies ownership. Tattooing or branding a person in the same way would be abhorrent, but this is a different kind of relationship. It is a different kind of belonging. It is a different kind of ownership. It ends in freedom, not slavery.

Belonging to God is true freedom. We already discussed that freedom to sin is not actual freedom, but slavery. God intended for the Israelites to be free. He desired freedom from oppression for them; they would have their own land. He also desired freedom from accusing law; they would have clear consciences and forgiveness of sins through faith in him. He desired freedom from death; they would have a resurrection to all eternity in him. All of this is from him. If they belonged to him, they would be truly free.

These words of blessing were a promise-Word. He would look upon his people; that is, he would not turn his loving gaze away from them. He would speak to them. It was the opposite of the silent treatment. We have all experienced a loved one turning his or her face from us. Maybe it was in disgust because of a harmful action or word. Maybe it was in disappointment because of a failure or mistake. It hurts. The relationship is harmed, even broken. "I can't even look at you right now" are words that penetrate like a dart into the soul. It is a devastating blow when God turns his gracious gaze from us. But God promised he would not. Instead, he turned from his own Son. Christ knew the answer to his own cry from the cross, "My God, my God, why have you forsaken me?" (Mark 15:34b). God turned from Christ because Christ became our sin. God was disgusted, disappointed, and ashamed of Christ instead of us.

The opposite of turning away is to look straight at a person. This too can be devastating. Think of Peter outside the high priest's courtyard during Jesus' trial. Jesus peered into his eyes after Peter denied even knowing Jesus (Luke 22:61). A parent's stare at a child might indicate, "I see you. I know what you have done." But it can also brighten a dark day. It says, "I love you. I delight in you. I want what is best for you." A smile indicates acceptance. It signifies belonging. God looked away from Christ so that he could look at you with delight. He sees Christ with your sin and sees you with Christ's righteousness. In illness, David cried out to God to turn to him: "Turn, LORD, and deliver me; save me because of your unfailing love" (Psalm 6:4). David is desperate and wants the Lord to look at him. "Turn, Lord!" Turn and look at me! Moses' face shone with the glory of God as he descended Mount Sinai (Exodus 34:29). This was both a fearful thing (God sees you) and also a glorious thing. Moses descended Mount Sinai with laws, glorious laws in which we delight. But as sinners they are a curse to us. So Moses' brother, Aaron, promised a delightful gaze from their fearsome Father, one of delight. "The LORD make his face shine on you and be gracious to you; the LORD turn his face toward you and give you peace" (Numbers 6:25,26). All will be right in Christ.

So the Israelites were marked again. Another promise-Word. More gospel. The relationship is one of a loving Father gazing adoringly at his innocent child, innocent in Christ. They would be protected. They would have freedom. They would always be *his*. They belonged. In Baptism we are marked, tattooed even, with the name of the triune God. We belong. We are protected. He will not turn his bright face away from us in disgust. He will always gaze lovingly upon us. We are forgiven. He will always see us as a father sees his newborn. The one he protects, loves, adores, and for whom he wants the best.

# 9.

# A WATER EISODUS

If an exodus is an exit, then an eisodus is an entrance. The exodus out of Egypt culminated with the eisodus, that is, the entrance into the Promised Land. Israel's 40-year journey was bookended with water: an exodus through the Red Sea and an eisodus through the Jordan River. The staff of Moses presided over the split of the Red Sea, but in the Jordan River God's throne would halt the river's stream. The priests walked the ark of the covenant into the riverbed and the water of the Jordan ceased to flow.

In preparation of their invasion of Canaan, the Israelites did their due diligence. They sent spies into Canaan on a reconnaissance mission. With help from Rahab they scouted out their God-given land for enemies of the Lord. The older generation continued their lack of faith in God's promise-Word and balked at the notion of fighting for the occupied land. Yet a remnant of the faithful always remained. So they began their invasion. They knew it would fail without God. Trust and water once again. They would go with God or not go at all.

The ark of the covenant was seen as God's throne. God "sat" on the cover of this box framed by gilded angels. This was God's presence among the Israelites. Yes, God is everywhere, but he also says, "Here is where I am" or better yet "Here is where I want you to find me." The ark of the covenant was housed in the special room in the tabernacle and, later, in the temple. God was in the Most Holy Place. Only the high priest would once a year enter this sanctuary of sanctuaries to make atonement for the people. But on occasion the ark of the covenant would venture out into the world. This was one of those times. The Israelites would quite literally follow God. They would go with God or not go at all.

Moses would not make the journey. He was a faithful leader, but he angered God by becoming angry at the people. He would get a glimpse of this Promised Land from Mount Nebo, but there he would die and be buried by the hand of God. Joshua would lead the people during the eisodus. Moses, the lawgiver, could not deliver the people into the Promised Land. God tabbed Joshua with this task.

Names matter, especially in the Bible. They carry meaning. Moses was called Moses because the Egyptian princess drew him from the Nile River as he floated by in a mini-ark made by his Hebrew mother, saving him from the infanticide of Hebrew boys ordered by the pharaoh. More water! Joshua's name is different. It is Hebrew. Joshua means "God is salvation" or "deliverance." It would be Joshua who would deliver Israel from danger to safety across the Jordan. Actually, it was God who delivered. It is God who saves. God is salvation.

The Greek version of the Hebrew name Joshua is Jesus. Jesus means "God is salvation." Jesus is Salvation. It is Jesus who crosses us over safely to the other side from our 40-year wilderness journey of trial to the land that flows with milk and honey. It is not Moses and his law but Jesus/Joshua and his gospel. It is not Moses and his failings into which we are baptized. We are baptized into Jesus, "God is Salvation."

Crossing Jordan has become a metaphor for crossing over from this life into the next. Elijah crossed over from west to east with his protégée, Elisha, to meet the horsemen of Israel and their chariots of fire. Elijah was whisked away into heaven as his coat (mantel) fell down (passed down) to Elisha as the main prophet of God in Israel. But the picture works both ways, not just from west to east but east to west. The Israelites crossed the Jordan River to receive their inheritance, their Promised Land. So when the time comes, we too will pass over from this world into our inheritance. And water will not be far from the picture. We are adopted in Baptism, made heirs of the kingdom. This is our land; it belongs to us. We have the deed, and the paperwork is written in blood and water. We cross Jordan.

# 10

# SPRINKLING OF BLOOD

Bloodstains. Any parent of a child knows grass stains and dirt stains. But blood? Blood is one of the toughest stains to get out. Yet the Bible tells us that blood cleanses. It is a striking image. How can blood, which stains, cleanse? This striking paradox was made visual in the liturgy of the Old Testament. Who could forget the blood smeared on the doorframes in Egypt? The priests sprinkled blood around the altar located in the tabernacle and then in the temple courtyard. On one occasion, Moses took blood and performed this ritual:

> Take the other ram, and Aaron and his sons shall lay their hands on its head. Slaughter it, take some of its blood and put it on the lobes of the right ears of Aaron and his sons, on the thumbs of their right hands, and on the big toes of their right feet. Then splash blood against the sides of the altar. And take some blood from the altar and some of the anointing oil and sprinkle it on Aaron and his garments and on his sons and their garments. Then he and his sons and their garments will be consecrated. (Exodus 29:19-21)

The priesthood of God was to be consecrated. The tabernacle and, later, the temple in which the priests made atonement for sin were also to be consecrated. Both the priests and the altar were to be set apart (consecrated) for something special. This was sacred business. The priests mediated between the Israelites and their God. The sinful Israelites could not enter the presence of God, not with their sin. Payment for sin was to be made. The priests were set apart from the nation to perform this task. They needed to be consecrated.

A covenant (a promise-Word) from God was given. It was a covenant in blood. Remember that the ancients cared about agreements more than we do. One indication of this was a ritual performed by God with Abram. A heifer, a goat, and a ram were each cut into two halves. An aisle was formed between the slaughtered halves of the animals. This ancient covenant practice was symbolic of the seriousness of covenants and oaths. The Hebrew for "make a covenant" is literally "cut a covenant," as in cut an animal into two pieces. The two parties of the covenant agreement, in this case God and Abram, walked through the space between the two halves of the sacrificed animals, no doubt, walking in blood. Although not explicitly mentioned in Genesis, the indication is obvious: The party that breaks the agreement ends up like the animals. Blood certainly adds some gravitas to the situation. Notice that God sealed the covenant by "walking" though the bloody aisle. A smoking firepot and blazing torch passed between the pieces (Genesis 15:17). But we do not read that Abram would walk through. In the end, this was a one-sided agreement. It was another promise-Word. All Abram was to do was to be still and take God at his word.

Aaron and the priests were consecrated in blood too. They were a part of this serious (blood-serious) covenant. It was a sacred duty. The altar at the temple that would wholly burn up sacrifices to God was sacred too. All were a symbol of the new covenant in the blood of Christ. God would provide the sacrifice, the blood, and the promise.

There is one more sprinkling of blood more striking than all the rest. On one occasion Moses sprinkles blood on the people (Exodus 24:8). Stop and ponder that scene for a moment. Can you imagine gathering before your leader and after he speaks and performs rituals, he turns to you and throws blood on you? Can you imagine droplets of blood hitting your face and staining your garments? Sacrifices were made to symbolize God's forgiveness. The blood on the people was also a part of this sacred agreement. The people "walked through." They made a promise to follow God's Word, and blood sealed the deal. But in the end their promises (and our promises) stink. This was about God consecrating his special people, setting them apart for a sacred duty to bring about the Messiah, their Savior. It was, finally, about cleansing them from sin. And it would, of course, be in blood.

Back to the paradox: They were cleansed with, of all things, blood. But isn't this the point? Water cannot wash away sin. A convicted felon cannot wash his hands and simply be acquitted of all charges. An abused woman can take a hundred showers, but that will not wash away what happened to her. No bath can wash away the shame, whether earned or not, whether because of sins committed or sins endured. Pilate tried to wash his hands of the injustice about to be carried out on Jesus of Nazareth, but the water running through his fingers could not atone for his cowardice, let alone the past sins of his life.

Nor can mere water wash away sin. The water needs the promise-Word. And the promise-Word is about a real historical event. A real sacrifice. Real justice. A real covenant in blood. The water needs the blood. It sounds so strange, grotesque even, but we should imagine the sprinkling of water on a child as a sprinkling of blood, sacred covenant blood. Christ's blood. That may take away from the precious cuteness of the baptismal event, but it makes it all the more poignant. Christ died for this child. Christ makes a covenant with this child. A promise-Word is spoken. The promise is written in blood. This is serious business.

The baptized receive a blood covenant with God. A promise-Word that he will not break. The baptized are saved and will always be loved by their protector-God. But they too are consecrated, that is, set apart for something holy. They will perform good deeds that God has prepared for them to accomplish (Ephesians 2:10). They too are priests who have direct access to God (1 Peter 2:5). They are to be God's ambassadors to the world, mediating, in a way, by proclaiming his promise-Word to the world.

## 11.

# WASHING RITUALS

The cleansing rituals of the Old Testament are peculiar to us living thousands of years later. They were commands from God through Moses that were to be kept. For example, a woman who gave birth was considered unclean for 40 days (40 again!). She could not enter the presence of God (at the temple) until her 40 days were up and she went through a cleansing ritual with the priests. We might wonder, What is the point of this? Didn't God preach against empty rituals such as these? (See, for example, Hosea 6:6.)

Before we go further into the explanation of these washing laws, we ought to examine the types of laws in the Old Testament. First, there is the moral law. This law always stands. It is always wrong to commit adultery. Even if there is no statute against adultery in a particular jurisdiction, it is still morally wrong. The second type of law is civil law. There is nothing inherently evil about driving a car on the right side or left side of a road. It is for the sake of order and safety that we have laws about which side of the road to drive on. Defiantly driving on the wrong side of the road only becomes a moral flaw because the driver is disobeying authority and putting people in danger.

Ceremonial law, the third type of law, is likewise not about morality or immorality in itself. These laws are cultural and catechetical. They bind people together (culture), and they teach a greater truth (catechesis). God commanded ceremonial laws to do both. The prohibitions against eating certain animals, the law of circumcision, and the washing rituals, not to mention the particular worship guidelines, all separated the Israelites from their neighbors culturally. Israel was different. Every culture is different, but Israel was really different. The Israelites believed in one God as opposed to many local deities. Their law code, although seemingly primitive compared to our modern norms, was progressive for the time. A cultural hedge was erected around Israel. They had a special mission to bring about the Messiah from their family, from their land. They needed to survive. The ceremonial laws helped build this hedge around Israel.

Maybe you are incredulous. How could culture protect a people? Isn't that the military's job? Certainly Israel defended itself with weapons, but military powers wax and wane. Borders shift. Governments change. Ancient peoples were routinely oppressed and oppressive. But cultural ties can outlast military victories and defeats. If you think this is implausible, watch a session of the United Nations. Where are the Midianites? Where is the Edomite ambassador, the Jebusite representative, or the Babylonian contingent? Those cultures are only found in the dustbin of history. Only the name Egypt remains from the time of Moses, and it is a wholly different culture today than the time of the pharaohs. But there is still an ambassador from Israel. It worked.

Many of the ceremonial laws provided a theological distinction between Israel and its neighbors. This is the catechetical, or teaching, aspect of the ceremonial laws.

Certain foods were off-limits to the Israelites. It protected their table. It is another aspect of ancient culture lost on us. Who you eat with matters. We actually do have a remnant of this in our current culture. Breaking bread with someone indicates at least some sort of tacit agreement. If the heads of state from two warring countries sit down for a state dinner, that has a profound effect on geopolitics and the stock market too! Remember, Israel was different. It had a special mission. Certainly other people could join the ranks of the Israelites and worship the true God, but it was the Israelites who would bring about the promised Messiah. They were not to eat with Gentiles.

The cleaning rituals provided a more personal theological lesson. Although we do not have a cheat sheet that fully explains the theological meaning of the cleansing rituals, we can easily see the parallels between cleanliness and righteousness on one hand and sin and uncleanness on the other hand. Some of the clean/ unclean laws were for safety. An Israelite with a skin disease was to be quarantined and only after being cured could the man or woman regain access to Israelite worship, and only after a washing ritual and inspection from the priests. It certainly hinted at sin (disease) but was also practical. Now think about other events that also made an Israelite unclean: contact with a corpse, a nocturnal emission, a woman's menstrual cycle, and giving birth all made a person "unclean." Notice that none of these can be avoided. Someone has to bury Grandma! Who could stop a menstrual cycle? And isn't giving birth a blessing?

Four lessons emerge. First, uncleanness is unavoidable. Second, many of the events that made a person unclean had to do with the cycle of life and death. Third, people cannot cleanse themselves. Finally, the priest must cleanse the person through a ritual act. Now think about sin. Is it not handed down through the generations (cycle of life)? Does it not end in death (cycle of life and death)? Is it not unavoidable? Can we get rid of it ourselves? Do we not need God to wash us from our sins? God gave the Israelites a daily catechism lesson in sin and grace.

Before we go any further, there is one more thing that is lost on our present-day minds: coming into the presence of God. We do not think in terms of sacred places, things, or events like the ancients did. In a way this is good. All is sacred because all is made by God and given back to us to use appropriately and enjoy. On the other hand, our spirituality seems to be detached from the physical. Philosophically we still think of ourselves in a modern way, that is, as thinking things. We are our brains. The ancients were more holistic. Our spirituality becomes independent of the physical and often of other people. It is overly personal and individualistic. It can at times dismiss the physical nature in which God comes to us and the physical church into which he has knitted us. It privileges the subjective over the objective and the spiritual over the physical.

This affects the way we think about coming into the presence of God. We have already stated that, yes, God is everywhere, but he also tells us that he will be in certain places for certain acts. We might have a spiritual feeling out in nature, but it is only with his physical Word, physical meal, physical washing, and through his physical church that we are forgiven. Left alone, the arrow points from us to God in worship rather than from God to us with a gift of forgiveness. There is no sacred space besides my heart. Not so for the Israelites. They came into the presence of God at the temple specifically for atonement. Not so for the new Israel either. God approaches us in his means of grace (Word, Holy Communion, Baptism, and Absolution).

There is an important theological nuance here. If I asked any Christian the question "Can sinners go to heaven?" all would answer, "Yes! Of course!" even if he or she might add a qualification like good works. But it is not true. Sinners cannot enter the holy presence of God. Sinners cannot go to heaven. If it were so, then it wouldn't be heaven anymore; it would be this world all over again with all of its flaws. The sinner must be made righteous. The sinner must be cleansed in order to enter the presence of God. Israel's washing rituals point to this theological fact.

The washing rituals of ancient Israel were foreshadows of Christ's washing and, in particular, Baptism. The baptized are cleansed. They are made righteous. They can enter the presence of God without fear of punishment. We are conceived in sin. We cannot help but be sinful. We cannot wash ourselves. God must wash us, and he does this through a ritual act. So Baptism is very much like the washing rituals of the Old Testament, but once again there is a fulfillment. The Old Testament washing rituals were shadows; baptism is the reality. Baptism is not an empty ritual; it actually delivers forgiveness. Baptism is not merely teaching; it is a deliverance.

# 12

# NAAMAN'S HUMBLING BATH

This distinction of clean or unclean reaches beyond the borders of Israel. It is a natural human desire to be clean, both outside and inside. There is also the obvious desire to be healthy. Life is a gift, and any threat to life is an attack from which we need to be defended. But our sinful hubris desires that we be the ones to cleanse ourselves. The story of Naaman and Elisha explores these very human desires (2 Kings 5).

Naaman was a great general for the king of Aram. He had notches on his belt from great military victories, many against lowly Israel. But even the greatest of men can be taken down by the smallest of things. Naaman had a skin disease. It must have bothered him to no end. Not just the literal irritation and threat of death, but the frustrating irritation that something unseen, something so small, could take down someone so big and powerful.

Another small thing would save him. A little girl. Unnamed. A slave captured from one of his raids of Israelite villages who now served his household. She told her master about a man of God back in her own country who could help: the irritable Elisha. So Naaman gathered the correct diplomatic "papers" and headed to Israel. It was not a raid or a reconnaissance mission but a humanitarian mission into foreign land. The king of the

Northern Kingdom (Israel) consented out of fear and let in the enemy.

Naaman and his entourage traveled to Elisha's home but were met with disrespect, or so they thought. Elisha did not even bother to leave his home to greet the great general. He only instructed the man of power to dip himself into the Jordan River seven times to cure his skin disease. Naaman was irate. Who did Elisha think he was? Were not the rivers of Aram greater than the Jordan? Aram had already proven itself mightier than Israel. Naaman's pride almost derailed the whole medical mission until his advisors seemed to say, "What do you have to lose?"

So Naaman entered the Jordan as instructed and he was cured. He tried to pay tribute materially to Elisha, but he would not accept. That's not how grace works. A rogue servant of Elisha named Gehazi tried to extort money from the now believing Naaman, but Gehazi was struck with leprosy for his greed. It's not how grace works.

Having someone wash you is humiliating. Helpless babies get bathed. Invalids need to be washed. It is sign of ineptitude, weakness, and helplessness. We cannot wash ourselves. Another must wash us. Naaman learned his lesson and faith was created: "Now I know that there is no God in all the world except in Israel" (2 Kings 5:15). It is a humbling thing to realize that we cannot help ourselves. It is a humbling thing to be washed by someone else. But we have no other avenue for salvation. We are trapped like Israel after escaping Egypt.

The pride of Naaman runs through all of us. So God has to humble us as he did Naaman. He does this with his law and even with suffering. If the goal is faith in Christ and the opposite of faith in Christ is faith in anything else (usually ourselves), then it seems to me that God must first beat the false faith (idolatry) out of us. We call this God's alien (or foreign) work. He does this so he can do his proper and true work of saving. If it takes leprosy, it will take leprosy. If it takes cancer, it will take cancer. Or a financial setback. Maybe a firing, an accident—I don't know, but I do know that even in the midst of heartache, frustration, and suffering, God has placed you where you need to be.

Doesn't this flip the script on pain and suffering? It provides meaning for something the rest of the world tries to dismiss as meaningless. If pain and suffering have no meaning, then half of life has no meaning and that's on a good day in a first world country, let alone a bad day in a third world country. I do not claim to have access to the mind of God; I only claim what God has spoken. Saint Paul wrote as only a person who has suffered could write:

> I consider that our present sufferings are not worth comparing with the glory that will be revealed in us. For the creation waits in eager expectation for the children of God to be revealed. For the creation was subjected to frustration, not by its own choice, but by the will of the one who subjected it, in hope that the creation itself will be liberated from its bondage to decay and brought into the freedom and glory of the children of God. And we know that in all things God works for the good of those who love him, who have been called according to his purpose. For those God foreknew he also

predestined to be conformed to the image of his Son, that he might be the firstborn among many brothers and sisters. And those he predestined, he also called; those he called, he also justified; those he justified, he also glorified. (Romans 8:18-21,28-30)

I cannot claim to know why a hurricane strikes a specific town on a specific day, nor do I know exactly why you are suffering what you suffer right now, but I do know that it will be for your good. It may be for no other reason than God is pushing you into a corner with nowhere to go but to him. God has you where you need to be, but not where you will always be.

Naaman learned this humbling lesson and so do we. We are always children, humbled, sometimes humiliated, but we are always the Father's children, adopted though the waters of Baptism. Washed in these saving waters as mothers bathe their little children. Humbling? Yes. Beautiful? Also yes.

# 13

# JOHN THE BAPTIZER

As we move from the Old Testament to the New Testament we see the pictures of water, blood, Baptism, and cleanliness become clearer. We arrive at the Jordan River and meet John the Baptist. John lived in the New Testament era, but he was Old Testament in character. He was a prophet. He pointed ahead to fulfillment. He even dressed the part, looking more like Elijah and Elisha than a first-century Jew of Palestine. He hung around the Jordan River preaching prophet's words. He dressed in sackcloth—a visual reminder of his repentant message. He ate locust and wild honey as if he was living in Elijah's famine. He was even executed by a king of Israel.

John prepared the way for Christ as the final "Old Testament" prophet. He himself was prophesized about in Isaiah: "A voice of one calling in the wilderness, 'Prepare the way for the Lord, make straight paths for him. Every valley shall be filled in, every mountain and hill made low. The crooked roads shall become straight, the rough ways smooth. And all people will see God's salvation'" (Luke 3:4-6).

John fulfilled this prophecy when he famously declared, "Look, the Lamb of God, who takes away the sin of the world! This is the one I meant when I said, 'A man who comes after me has surpassed me because he was before me.' I myself did not know him, but the reason I came baptizing with water was that he might be revealed to Israel" (John 1:29-31). John prepared the road for the King of kings as anybody in the ancient world might. The road was cleared and made level to make the King's entrance smooth. But this was not about road grading. It was about preparing hearts.

A believing heart must know that it needs saving. If a person does not believe that he or she needs saving, he or she will reject the help. So John preached fire. He called those who came to leer at his baptisms in the Jordan River a "brood of vipers" (Luke 3:7). He wondered out loud who warned them about the coming wrath (a reference to the coming of Jesus). Jesus' entrance into this world is wrath to those who reject him, but sweet grace to those who trust him. As was stated earlier, God must do his alien work first.

God's alien work results in repentance. *Repentance* is a funny word. It means "to turn." In this case it means to turn *from* sin and turn *to* God. The problem is that a sinner cannot turn to God. In the end God works the turning. Repentance is a part of faith and faith is a gift of God. So John's ministry was a ministry of preparation, and his baptism was a baptism of repentance. One who follows will actually forgive. Jesus' baptism is one of fire in which he burns the chaff (sin) and keeps the grain (saint). It is circumcision of the heart. It is a death of the old and the resurrection of the new. John was the last Old Testament character because he was still looking ahead to the fulfillment. Jesus will actually forgive.

It is once again about God forgiving and granting faith to the dead in sin. For those baptized into John and not Christ, it is still about faith in the Coming One. For those baptized in Christ, it is the real deal. The preparation is the same. Stop trusting yourself and trust in God. If you trust in yourself, you cannot trust in God. There is no middle ground. John's baptism was the last in a long line of water events and washings that all pointed to the real deal, Christ. So we end the preparation and move on to the real deal.

# 14.

# THE BAPTISM OF OUR LORD

All three persons of the Holy Trinity were present and active at creation, and all three were present and active at the Jordan River when John baptized Jesus. Once again water is present and so are heavenly words. This was an inauguration of sorts for Jesus of Nazareth. He was begotten from the Father and truly divine from all eternity, but now it was announced to the world in a unique way that he was the Father's Son. The Father bellowed from heaven, "You are my Son, whom I love; with you I am well pleased" (Luke 3:22). The Father gave his approval. This is the guy. This is the long-awaited one. He is finally here. He will do my bidding. I am pleased with him. Every inclination of his heart is pure all of the time. He is the perfect one. He is the righteous one. He has come to be the fulfillment of God's promise-Word.

The Holy Spirit flutters once again, this time as a dove, a symbol of peace. The fire of John's preaching was now a refining fire. It made souls pure. It gave souls peace. Peace on earth, peace forever in heaven, and peace in the souls of terrified sinners. The Holy Spirit proceeds from the Father to the Son in this special event that serves as the beginning of Christ's ministry on earth. He enters the office of the Messiah, that is, the Christ, the Anointed One.

This water event marks another beginning, this time not the beginning of creation but the beginning of the redemption of creation. Jesus is a prophet, but a different kind of prophet. He not only speaks the Word of God; he is the Word of God. He is commissioned as prophet-missionary. The eternal Logos who orders all things now walks the earth in flesh to speak love to disordered people. The disorder of sin is set right by the order of the Logos, the Savior. Christ's baptism is his commissioning as a prophet-missionary who brings good news.

Jesus is also our High Priest, but not in the order of the law, the Levitical priesthood. Like John the Baptist, the Levitical priesthood was a placeholder, a foreshadow of one to come. The sons of Levi made sacrifices to atone for sin, but these sacrifices were only a picture of the true sacrifice to come. Jesus is in the line of a more ancient priestly order, the order of Melchizedek (Hebrews 7). Jesus' priesthood is one of grace. Like all priests he serves as a mediator between sinful people and God with a sacrifice. However, Jesus is different because he is God, and since he is God there is no separation from the people and God. God comes to us. There is no middleman. The "mediator" is God. But there is more. He is not only the priest who makes the mediating sacrifice to God, but he is also the sacrifice himself. He is the sacrificing Priest and the sacrifice. His baptism is his ordination into this high priestly order.

Yet there remains an unanswered question, one John posed to Jesus: Why should Jesus, the perfect one, be baptized? Shouldn't Jesus wash John and not the other way around? From what does Jesus need to be cleansed? Jesus replies with a cryptic answer to John's inquiry: "To fulfill

all righteousness" (Matthew 3:15). But what does that mean? In the end we go back to the reason Christ was inaugurated into the office of the Christ. He is the one who would become sin for us and then give us his righteousness (2 Corinthians 5:21). He is the High Priest who is not unsympathetic with the plight of sinful humans. He is tempted in every way we are except without sin (Hebrews 4:15). He came here to save, and in order to save us he needed to take our sins. He is both Priest and sacrifice.

This is why he must be fully human. If sinners need his righteousness, then his righteousness needs to be legitimate. So what if God comes down here and is perfect? He's God! It is not a great feat for the divine to be perfect. "Walk a mile in our shoes," we might protest. But what if God did walk in our shoes? What if he had the same struggles and the same bodily urges and the same obstacles as us? Well, he did. His righteousness is legitimate. He turned the other cheek when we sought revenge. He spoke love when we spewed venom. He obeyed when we disobeyed. He offered compassion when we offered spite.

He also needs to be truly divine. Who else could be perfect in a sinful world? And the sad truth is that plenty of people have died for you and me, many for our freedom, but who of them could free us from death, let alone eternal punishment? Only God. Only the God-man. Only the High Priest. Only Christ. He went into the Jordan River willingly to put himself into this mission. He would become sin for us and we would become his righteousness.

So God becomes man. So Jesus is born in Bethlehem. So the carpenter's son from Nazareth suffers. So

the Christ is handed over to the hands of men—falsely accused, arrested, tried, tortured, crucified, and buried. So the same Christ preaches and teaches, performs miracles, rises and ascends, rules all things, and will return. So Jesus gets baptized. Why? Why any of it? Why all of it? To fulfill all righteousness, that's why.

# 15

# THE BAPTISMAL LIFE

These biblical water stories come to their fulfillment both in the Jordan River and at Calvary, at the baptism of our Lord and then later at his crucifixion. The washing means nothing without the dying. The water means nothing without the blood. None of this comes to us without the promise-Word, and the Word is only active because of the Spirit. Water and blood, Word and Spirit—just like at the beginning, just like the whole of the Old Testament.

Now the story is your story. The water story jumps off the pages of Holy Scripture and into your life. The water and the blood. The Word and the Spirit. Even the dying and the rising. Baptism is a death and a resurrection. It is the death of the sinful nature and a resurrection of the new creation. It is your death and resurrection into Christ. Saint Paul makes it explicit:

> Don't you know that all of us who were baptized into Christ Jesus were baptized into his death? We were therefore buried with him through baptism into death in order that, just as Christ was raised from the dead through the glory of the Father, we too may live a new life. For if we have been united with him in a death like his, we will certainly also

be united with him in a resurrection like his. For we know that our old self was crucified with him so that the body ruled by sin might be done away with, that we should no longer be slaves to sin— because anyone who has died has been set free from sin. Now if we died with Christ, we believe that we will also live with him. For we know that since Christ was raised from the dead, he cannot die again; death no longer has mastery over him. The death he died, he died to sin once for all; but the life he lives, he lives to God. In the same way, count yourselves dead to sin but alive to God in Christ Jesus. (Romans 6:3-11).

Your baptism was a crucifixion. Your baptism was a death and burial too. Your baptism was also a resurrection into a new life. You are made a part of the story.

Christ makes you his. He pulls you into his life. He makes you a part of his death, burial, and resurrection. He is intimate with you. What could be more intimate than being buried and rising with someone? His story is your story, and it is a violent one. There had to be a death. There is no such thing as reforming a sinner. If that were the goal, then the result would be nothing more than a reformed sinner, and sinners don't go to heaven. God wants nothing to do with sinners. So he needs to kill. There has to be a death and a resurrection. So he kills you. He kills you to make you alive. But notice the intimacy: He dies with you. You are not alone, not even in death.

So when it comes time for your earthly death you may say to yourself, "Ha! This is old hat for me. I already died. I was crucified, in fact. I was buried and I came through the other side with a resurrection." Death no longer has mastery over you. Satan, the accuser, can no longer bring charges against you. You are dead to sin and resurrected as something new. No accusation can touch you, and therefore the punishment for sin (death) no longer is your master.

This is true confidence. This is the confidence of a Christian funeral. A good Christian funeral is not merely a memorial service. That is too small a thing for those who have already been crucified, buried, and resurrected with Christ. We should never be satisfied with mere memories of those who have physically died. This is a trick of Satan. He wants us to be satisfied with a celebration of life or some sort of thing. He wants to soothe us with a false comfort. He wants us to settle for sweet-smelling flowers, old pictures, and shared memories. "Not good enough!" yells the Christian. "Not good enough!" We do not bury reformed sinners; we only lay to rest those we will see again. We believe in a resurrection. We will never be satisfied with memories. We dare to say, "We will see you again!"

We carry this profound confidence on our hearts and in our mouths because we have already died. "Don't you know? Don't you know that the baptized have already died? This is old hat! This loved one has already been through a crucifixion and came out the other side alive in Christ. What can a physical death do to this child of God? Nothing!" We boldly assert the confidence of 1 Corinthians chapter 15:

> When the perishable has been clothed with the imperishable, and the mortal with immortality,

then the saying that is written will come true: "Death has been swallowed up in victory."

"Where, O death, is your victory? Where, O death, is your sting?"

The sting of death is sin, and the power of sin is the law. (1 Corinthians 15:54-56)

Even with tears in our eyes, we point a defying finger into the face of death and the devil and say, "You can't have him." Or "She doesn't belong to you." And "You can't have me. I don't belong to you. I will live." It is the confidence of Job: "I know that my redeemer lives, and that in the end he will stand on the earth. And after my skin has been destroyed, yet in my flesh I will see God; I myself will see him with my own eyes—I, and not another. How my heart yearns within me!" (Job 19:25-27).

All this because of Baptism.

This confidence is not only for the moment we bury a loved one or face our own mortality. It is for every day. Every day is a new day. Every day is new because we are dead to sin and resurrected into life. Take your baptismal certificate and hang it on your bedroom wall—right by your door. Take it out of your mother's scrapbook. It belongs to you. It is not a memory of the past; it is a daily reminder. More than that, it is proof of your identity. You are a baptized child of God. You have been through death and back with Christ. You may not remember that violent baptism, but it happened and your baptism certificate reminds you not only of the past but also your present reality. This is who you are: redeemed in Christ.

Look at that certificate every day with confidence. Say to the world, "Bring it on! What do you have for me today? It might be failure. It might be pestilence. It might be a sorrow I have not yet felt. It may be famine, ruin, pain, or even death. You might try to overcome me today, world, but you cannot take away the historical reality that I was baptized. You cannot unring this bell. My baptism was a real-life, historical event just as real as yesterday's stock prices, baseball scores, and weather. You cannot take away my baptism!"

Your intimate connection with Christ in his crucifixion and his resurrection gives you permission to enter the darkness. You may wake up and be Job tomorrow. You may lose your health and your wealth; you may bury your children or be struck with a seemingly incurable disease. You may die. But so what? You already died. You already rose. You already have heaven. So bring it on, world! Christ says to you, "We have already been through worse. You were already crucified with me and we came out the other side with a resurrection to a new life. What could be worse? What could touch you now? Come with me through this cross. If you have already been through my cross with me, what can this cross of suffering do to you now? I give you permission to enter the darkness. Come with me."

This intimate connection with Christ was solidified at your baptism, but it harkens back to Christ's own baptism. Martin Luther put it poetically in his famous "flood prayer":

> Almighty, eternal God, who according to your
> strict judgment condemned the unbelieving

world through the flood and according to your great mercy preserved believing Noah and the seven members of his family, and who drowned Pharaoh with his army in the Red Sea and led your people Israel through the same sea on dry ground, thereby prefiguring this bath of your Holy Baptism, and who through the baptism of your dear child, our LORD Jesus Christ, hallowed and set apart the Jordan and all water to be a blessed flood and a rich washing away of sins: we ask for the sake of this very same boundless mercy of yours that you would graciously look upon N. and bless him with true faith in the Holy Spirit so that through this same saving flood all that has been born in him from Adam and whatever he has added thereto may be drowned in him and sink, and that he, separated from the number of the unbelieving, may be preserved dry and secure in the holy ark of the Christian church and may at times fervent in spirit and joyful in hope serve your name, so that with all believers in your promise he may become worthy to attain eternal life through Jesus Christ our Lord. Amen.[3]

Luther connects a series of Old Testament water events to Baptism, even of Jesus in the Jordan River. Let

---

[3]Small Catechism, Baptismal Booklet: 14, *The Book of Concord: The Confessions of the Evangelical Lutheran Church*, edited by Robert Kolb and Timothy J. Wengert (Minneapolis: Augsburg Fortress, 2000), pp. 373-744. See also "Sermon at the Baptism of Bernhard Von Anhalt, 1540," *Luther's Works*, American Edition, Vol. 51 (Philadelphia: Fortress Press, 1959), pp. 315-329.

me put it less poetically: Jesus exchanges his righteousness for sin, and it occurs at the cross and is delivered at Baptism. He sanctifies the waters of Baptism.[4] He makes them efficacious. Jesus goes into the waters of Baptism with his righteousness, and we enter with our sin. We come out with his righteousness, and Jesus takes our sin to the cross. To put it even more crassly, Jesus is like OxiClean. He enters the water as the cleaning agent, and we are the dirty socks, but we emerge clean, and he emerges with our sin. While we must be careful not to put on a meaning to Scripture that is not there, this analogy is descriptive. Baptism is where we die and rise. It is where our sins are washed away and we are made righteous. None of this works unless Christ brings his righteousness to us. Baptism, as a means by which God delivers grace, delivers this happy exchange of sin for righteousness. You are righteous in Christ. This is who you are now. You are redeemed in Christ. So bring it on, world!

---

[4]Luther's statement that Jesus sanctifies the waters of Baptism is not to say that the water of Baptism has a magical power. This is poetical but instructive language. While this language might be foreign to our modern ears, we can charitably understand Luther's point here: Jesus' righteousness is what makes Baptism salvific. Baptism is a means of grace. This is how he delivers forgiveness to poor sinners. This is the "happy exchange," that is, Christ exchanges his righteousness for our sin (2 Corinthians 5:21).

## 16.

# A REPENTANT LIFE

The Christian life is a baptismal life, and the baptismal life is a repentant life. We have already stated that repentance, true repentance, is simply faith. It is a turning *from* sin and *to* God. It is the desire to no longer be a sinner, but to be righteous in Christ. This is the act of God. He does the turning. He "repents" you. Who else would do it? Us? We are dead to sin. The dead cannot do anything (Romans 6,7). Another way to picture this is with the death and resurrection reality found in Baptism. The old is killed; the new is resurrected. John's baptism of repentance in the Jordan River gives way to Christ's baptism of renewal. Now it is reality. Not just a death but a resurrection. We anticipate no longer. We live in the reality right now.

Baptism is a onetime event, but it is also a daily event. There is no need to baptize more than once. God made a promise and he keeps his promises. He doesn't need to baptize you again. We only take him at his word, his promise-Word. It is like an adopted child. The baptized are adopted into the family of God. We are granted the full rights of sonship. This picture of sonship in the ancient world carried more weight than it does for us today. To be a son meant to be an heir. You were a freeman, not a servant. You were the legal heir to the estate.

So when we are baptized, we are given the legal right to the estate of heaven. Whether free or slave, Jew or Gentile, male or female, we are all made *sons* in the ancient inheritance system (Galatians 3:26).

This legal right cannot be taken from us. We can forfeit this right, I suppose. It is possible. We can run away from the family, but the adoption still stands. We prodigal children may deny our family, live a lifestyle wholly contradictory to our family values. We may soil the family name and reject the family's love, but if one day we return and knock on the door, the family accepts us. In this analogy of sonship it is even more stark: We have the legal right to the estate.

Permit me a tangent. Many parents worry about their children, especially the children who grow in age but not in maturity. What will happen to them? Will they make it in life? Many Christian parents have spent sleepless nights wondering about the faith of their prodigal children. Will they lose their faith? What will happen to them not just in this world, but in the next? Yes, it is possible and certainly has happened that a person loses his or her faith. But God made a promise. The prodigal children can try to outrun God, but my bet is on God. The Good Shepherd leaves the flock of 99 to track down the 1. So worried parents of the baptized, know this: Our God is a gracious God, and he made a promise, a baptismal promise.

Baptism is a onetime event. God doesn't need to do it again. He gave his word. Take him at his word. But Baptism is an ongoing reality as well. It is repeated, so to speak, each time the law pierces sinful souls and the gospel soothes those same sinful souls. Every time God performs his alien work on us, whether it be his accusing law or through suffering, he kills us. And every time he performs his proper work on us, that is, preaching the good news of forgiveness, he makes us alive in him. This is a miracle, for the dead cannot raise themselves.

This is your daily baptismal reality. The baptismal life is a life of constant dying and rising. When you look at your baptismal certificate and say, "Bring it on, world! You can take everything from me, but you can't undo my baptism," you can also say, "I am not the sinful person I was yesterday. I am new. I am new in Christ. The old person died; a new person has risen." Your baptism makes you who you are. This is your true identity. Who you are now and who you will be for all eternity: righteous in Christ.

However, on this side of heaven you are still a sinner. You are a sinner-saint; that is, you are simultaneously a sinner and a saint. You are 100 percent sinner and 100 percent saint all at the same time. The math doesn't work out, but it sure explains my life and your life too. How can we be so selfish one moment and gracious the next? How can we be so humble one moment and so full of hubris the next? So we go to bed with regret, but we know tomorrow is a new day. Every day is a new day for the baptized. And we wake up into baptismal reality. It's not who we are anymore. The old is gone and the new has arrived. And then we do it all over again. Sinner-saints. Alien work and proper work. Law and gospel. Death and resurrection. Until one day the cycle is broken and we emerge as a saint in heaven without threat of sin. "If we have been united with him in a death like his, we will certainly also be united with him in a resurrection like his" (Romans 6:5).

# 17

# A HUMBLED LIFE

The Christian life is a baptismal life. The baptismal life is a repentant life. The repentant life is a humbling life. It is not a flashy life, this baptismal life. It is as gritty as our God. God has a standard *modus operandi*. He tends to use the ordinary to accomplish the extraordinary. But not always. Sometimes there is thunder and lightning. Sometimes water turns into wine. Sometimes the sun stops and waves are silenced, but generally God uses ordinary means. In this way he continues to be intimate with us.

Naaman found this out the hard way. He wanted a grandiose scene. He wanted a healing. He wanted something big and epic that fit his life as a general in the army of Aram. He was important and so he demanded importance. But Elisha wouldn't even venture out of his home to greet the great general. Elisha only told him to dip himself seven times in the Jordan River. How insulting to the great soldier!

The humility was not Naaman's but God's. It was God who stooped low, not Naaman. And it was Naaman's honor to be washed by God, not God's honor to wash Naaman. John the Baptist got it right and wrong in that same Jordan River. Jesus should have baptized John, not the other way around, but John missed the point even if he was correct. This is how God operates. This is his

MO. He hides himself in the ordinary to accomplish the extraordinary. He does it because of love. Jesus dipped himself into the same lowly Jordan River that Naaman did centuries earlier. He did this to fulfill all righteousness, a righteousness he gifts to us.

Should only the rich and powerful have God's washing, dear Naaman? Should salvation only be grandiose? Should it come with gold and silver and not in muddy waters? God needed to do his alien work on Naaman first. God needed to humble Naaman. God needed to show Naaman that he wasn't that great, that he was helpless, in fact. Naaman needed God's law. "You can't do it. You never could. You never will. You need me and this is how I come to you. In water. Ordinary water." Then, and only then, did God come and wash the desperate Naaman. God did not cleanse Naaman because Naaman was important but because Naaman was helpless. A doctor does not treat the healthy (Luke 5:31). God does not need to save the righteous.

God's desire is that all repent and turn to him. So he repents us. We stubbornly resist, but he gets his people sooner or later. Another way to say this is that God is evangelical. This means that he is about the gospel. It is what *evangelical* means. He desires our salvation. If God desires the salvation of people who cannot save themselves, then he must do the work. He comes to us, not the other way around. It is not God's honor to wash us. It is our honor to be washed.

If God is evangelical, then he is incarnational in the sense that we cannot go to him. So he comes to us. And if he is incarnational, that is, he comes to us in the flesh, then it makes sense that he would continue to come to us in real, tangible, physical ways. We do not climb a high mountain to find the answer to life. We do not have to reach some sort of enlightenment to know God. He does not zap us with special knowledge. He gives us his Word. And this Word is tangible. It is written and spoken. It is ink on a page. It travels on airwaves and beats upon eardrums. It is physical. He uses mere paper and ink. He uses flawed preachers and sinful parents to speak words of grace to children. It is his MO—the ordinary to accomplish the extraordinary. He comes to us in ordinary means.

Humbled Naaman entered the muddy waters of the Jordan River in front of his entourage. The great general presumably stripped down to his undergarments, a truly humiliating experience for any ancient male, let alone a great general. So it is with the water poured over the head of a whimpering infant or an emotional adult bending over a font in front of friends and family. It is both humbling and a great honor to be washed by God. He hides in ordinary means to bring about epic events.

Our God is a hidden God (Isaiah 45:15). He hides because his glory would blow us away. It is an act of grace. He also hides so that he can be close. This is a paradox: He hides to be revealed. God hides so that we do not try to find him where he does not want to be found. He hides so that we find him where he wants to be found. For example, he does not want to be found primarily in nature. There we might find the glory of God, but only in his power and inevitably only his law. Sure, his creation is beautiful, but it is also terrifying. The snowcapped mountains are gorgeous from a distance but can be treacherous if you are stuck in an avalanche. Who of us does not wonder at a summer storm? Who of us has not taken cover because of a storm? If we only seek God in nature, we only are left, in the end, with his raw power. A power that seems to indiscriminately punish and reward both the wicked and the righteous.

God hides in places where he wants us to find him. In those places we see both his law and his gospel. We see that his true glory is love, not his ability to wow us with great feats of might. And where he is most hidden is the place where he is the most revealed: the cross. At the cross we see how serious God is about sin. There must be a death. At the cross we see how serious he is about his mercy. It will be his death, not ours. He continues this hidden-to-be-revealed *modus operandi* in Baptism. It is mere water and his Word, but it will guarantee heaven for the washed.

Have you ever wondered why Jesus often told eye-witnesses to his miracles not to tell anybody what they saw? It seems counterintuitive until you ponder the paradox of the hidden God: he hides to be revealed. God desires to be found and to be known on his own terms. So he often told the eyewitnesses to keep their mouths shut. He didn't want to be known as the miracle worker as much as he needed to be known as the crucified. He also wants to deal with us primarily with words. We are to take God at his word. Faith comes from hearing the Word. It might seem counterintuitive to halt the news of his miracles (as if the people were not going to blab anyway), but he knew that it was about not just publicity but the right kind of message, a crucifixion message.

Jesus may not come to you through a spectacular miracle; in fact, that is probably very unlikely, but so what? This is not his typical MO. He hides. You might wonder, *Where is God in my life?* as you wait for a miracle or some spectacular turn of events, but you seek God where he does not desire to be found. Where is God? Once again we see God's gracious intimacy with us. In the baptismal life, God is never far away. His adoption promise is always with us. He knows our names. He dies with us and rises with us. He washes us. He is intimate with us. How could he ever get closer to us than that?

## 18.

# WATER EVERYWHERE

Water is everywhere in Scripture, and water is everywhere in your life. The washing rituals of the Old Testament were daily catechism lessons for the Israelites. The Israelites were profoundly reminded that they were sinful, that sin was passed down through birth and ended in death, that they could not help but be sinful, that they could not cleanse themselves, that they needed an outside source to cleanse them, and that this cleansing came through a ritual.

Baptism too is a ritual performed by someone else upon us. We too are sinful from conception, and this sin ends in death. It is a ritual, but not an empty one. It is the real deal. One and done. No need to wash again (John 13:10). We are washed. Period. Yet we also notice that Baptism is a death and resurrection thing. This death and resurrection occur when we are hammered with God's law and made alive in Christ. It is at once a onetime event and a continuing reality. The ancient Israelites were given a daily catechism lesson of this sin-grace reality through the clean/unclean distinctions and ceremonial washing rituals. But what about us?

Look around and notice the water around you. Not a day goes by that water is not a part of your life. Even if you would be stranded in the middle of the desert, water would be on your mind (even more than if you had easy access to water). It is not too corny, I hope, that when you take a shower, turn on the spigot to water plants, or pour yourself a glass of water, Baptism comes to mind. Jesus is the Water of Life that ends all thirst. Jesus washed you in Baptism so that you could enter heaven. Water is everywhere in the baptismal life. It is dripping wet.

So is the desire to be clean. This is also a daily reality. We need to wash our hands for health, and we need to wash our bodies for the same reason and also to feel refreshed. But we desire not only an outward cleanliness but also an inward cleanliness. Nobody wakes up in the morning and hopes to be impure, to be haunted by past mistakes, or to feel the guilt of a dirty sin. It was mentioned previously that this is true of both sins committed by us and sins committed against us. The abused cannot wash away the abuse no matter how many showers are taken. Sinners cannot rid themselves of the guilt no matter how many times they wash their hands. Baptism is the antidote to this sense of uncleanness.

The hard truth remains, though, that we are sinners. We are unclean and we know it. More than that, we feel it. This is the daily struggle of sinner-saints. The death and resurrection cycle is also a clean-unclean cycle. A life of spiritual battle emerges. Two entities vie for control: the devil and God. Paul put it this way:

> We know that the law is spiritual; but I am unspiritual, sold as a slave to sin. I do not understand what I do. For what I want to do I do not do, but what I hate I do. And if I do what I do not want to do, I agree that the law is good. As

it is, it is no longer I myself who do it, but it is sin living in me. For I know that good itself does not dwell in me, that is, in my sinful nature. For I have the desire to do what is good, but I cannot carry it out. For I do not do the good I want to do, but the evil I do not want to do—this I keep on doing. Now if I do what I do not want to do, it is no longer I who do it, but it is sin living in me that does it. So I find this law at work: Although I want to do good, evil is right there with me. For in my inner being I delight in God's law; but I see another law at work in me, waging war against the law of my mind and making me a prisoner of the law of sin at work within me. What a wretched man I am! Who will rescue me from this body that is subject to death? Thanks be to God, who delivers me through Jesus Christ our Lord! So then, I myself in my mind am a slave to God's law, but in my sinful nature a slave to the law of sin. (Romans 7:14-25)

Sinner-saints battle every single day of their lives. A sinner is drowned in the waters of Baptism, but, as they say, the old guy can still swim. And the battle continues until kingdom come. But do not worry, dear combatants of this spiritual war, you are not just soldiers in this battle, but you are the prize of this battle. It is Christ who wars for you, and he already won.

So every day we put on the armor of God (Ephesians 6:10-18) to do battle, but we know the outcome. Battles will be lost, but the war is already won. We fight with the Word as our sword that speaks truth to us against the lies of the world that we are not saved, that we need to do more, or, worse, that we do not need God's help. We hold up our shield of faith as we trust God to protect us from the flaming arrows of the devil's temptation to trust in ourselves. Our belt is the truth of God's Word that holds it all together and protects our most vulnerable parts. Our breastplate is the righteousness of Christ that protects our hearts from the accusations of Satan. Our helmet is salvation in Christ that protects our crown, and our feet are ready to go out into the world with the peace of the gospel for our comfort and the comfort of all we meet.

This armor is on you through your baptism. It is your protection. You have access and the right to all that God provides. You are his dear child. You may not see the armor, but you see the water. May it be a reminder to you not only of this daily spiritual battle between old and new, between Satan and Christ, but also that the battle has already been won. It is not just a faucet from which you drink; you drink from the well of life. It is not just your hands that are washed in the sink; you are washed by God. It is not just water that it necessary for your earthly life; it is water that gives you eternal life. Water is everywhere, as are the reminders of your salvation in Christ.

# 19.

# THE BLOOD AND THE WATER TESTIFY

It all comes together on the cross. This is where the hidden God is the most revealed. This is where salvation is won. This is where sins are paid for. This is where the sinner dies. This is where Christ pulls the baptized into his life. This is where we see blood—blood and water.

John the evangelist wrote this beautiful paragraph in his first letter:

> This is the one who came by water and blood—Jesus Christ. He did not come by water only, but by water and blood. And it is the Spirit who testifies, because the Spirit is the truth. For there are three that testify: the Spirit, the water and the blood; and the three are in agreement. We accept human testimony, but God's testimony is greater because it is the testimony of God, which he has given about his Son. Whoever believes in the Son of God accepts this testimony. Whoever does not believe God has made him out to be a liar, because they have not believed the testimony God has given about his Son. And this is the testimony: God has given us eternal life, and this

life is in his Son. Whoever has the Son has life; whoever does not have the Son of God does not have life. (1 John 5:6-12)

Once again we hear about water, blood, Word, and Spirit. Old Testament law required "two or three witnesses" for evidence in legal cases, especially capital crimes (Deuteronomy 17:6 and 19:5). Perhaps this was on John's mind when he wrote that "the three are in agreement," the Spirit, the water, and the blood. The water of Christ's baptism testifies to his divinity (he is the Father's Son) and to his mission (the Father is pleased with his Son). The blood of the cross testifies to the completion of his mission ("It is finished"). And the Spirit, of course, is the one who inspires the prophets of old and the apostles of the New Testament. They agree: Jesus is true man and true God, Savior of the world, and lover of sinners.

John also tells us in his gospel that the soldiers pierced the side of Jesus instead of their regular custom of breaking the legs of their victim. The pointed spear brought "a sudden flow of blood and water" (John 19:34). John connects this with testimony (Word): "The man who saw it has given testimony, and his testimony is true. He knows that he tells the truth, and he testifies so that you also may believe" (John 19:35). John's passionate testimony was eyewitness testimony. He saw the blood. He saw the blood and water. He heard the voice of Christ, and now his voice testifies to this truth. Jesus is Lord and Savior. John knew this because of the Spirit and his Word. He knew because of the blood and the water. They all are in agreement.

No one who knew the story of the Exodus could miss the connection. Jesus is the true Passover Lamb. The lambs slaughtered in Egypt could not have broken bones. They were to be perfect. No blemish, no broken bones. Jesus needed to be perfect. So when the soldiers came to do their dirty work—break the bones of the criminals to quicken their deaths—they noticed that Jesus had already given up his spirit. To make sure that he was dead, they pierced him. The perfect Passover Lamb's bones were not broken, "but he was pierced for our transgressions" (Isaiah 53:5). The wrath of God would pass over us sinners, and the stroke of justice would strike the Lamb just as the angel of the Lord passed over those ancient Israelite homes (Exodus 12:23).

Blood is powerful. It can testify. Christ's blood testified his love to the world. The crucifixes and crosses hanging in churches, hung around necks, and found in great works of art today still testify to this gracious love. The testimony is this: "The Lamb of God has taken away the sins of the world. And these who are marked as ones redeemed by Christ crucified are made pure in blood."

Moses sprinkled blood on the people (Exodus 24:8). The blood testified about the covenant that God made with his people. The blood testified. This was not the first time blood testified. Abel's blood cried out for justice. The blood of Jesus speaks a "better word than the blood of Abel" (Hebrews 12:24). Moses' sprinkling pointed ahead to the blood and the water, to the cross, and to Baptism. Abel's blood only groaned in pain, just as this world groans in anticipation of something better (Romans 8:22), but Christ's blood brings true justice and ends the pain.

Moses sprinkled blood on the people, but Jesus would wash with his blood. It marks Christians as washed. It testifies. And so does the water. Blood is not sprinkled on the people anymore, but water is. The water testifies and its testimony is the same: this one is washed in Christ. It is a bloody Baptism even if there is no blood. It's a Passover testimony even if there is no slaughtered lamb or unleavened bread. Your baptismal certificate testifies to you. Watery remembrances of Baptism testify to you. The Spirit and the water and the blood all testify with words to you. They give you a promise-Word. And the Spirit and the water and the blood all agree: You are washed clean in Christ.

## 20.

# CROSSING JORDAN

The law cannot get you into heaven; only the gospel can accomplish this feat. You cannot earn the favor of God with your life. Who can be perfect? Not only that, but this heavenly gift would not be a gift if it had to be earned. It would no longer be a gift but an obligation God must fulfill. It would be a quid pro quo relationship; that is, we do something for God and then he is obligated to do something for us in return. That is not a Father-child relationship of love but a business arrangement. Then what of Christ? If we could earn salvation, then Christ died for nothing (Galatians 2:21).

Moses the lawgiver did not lead Israel into the Promised Land. It had to be Joshua, "God is salvation." It had to be Joshua, whose name in Greek is Jesus. It is Jesus who will lead us into the promised land of heaven after fighting off the devil's temptations in the Transjordan wilderness. Jesus did what we cannot do. Jesus did what Moses could not do. Jesus did what the law could not do for us.

The Jordan River is a special place. Readers of the Bible don't travel very far through the pages of Scripture without coming across this body of water. Lot chose the plain of Jordan as his land (Genesis 13:10,11). Jacob met Esau after crossing Jordan (Genesis 32:10). Jacob was buried near the river (Genesis 50:10). The Israelites camped near the Jordan River, looking longingly across it (Numbers 31:12). Joshua led the people across Jordan (Joshua 3). Elijah and Elisha crossed the Jordan for Elijah's farewell (2 Kings 2:1-18), and Naaman was washed in its waters (2 Kings 5). It is also where John baptized and Jesus was inaugurated (Matthew 3).

The Jordan River provided a sense of boundary as do many bodies of water. It was often the eastern boundary of Israel. It separated Israel from the nations. The river also was a symbolic boundary. It symbolized the boundary of clean and unclean (Israel and the gentile nations). The closer one approached the ark of the covenant in the Most Holy Place of the temple, the closer that person came to God. As a person drew closer to a holy God, there were a series of boundaries, each signifying more holiness, that is, being set apart for something special. The Most Holy Place, the Holy Place, the temple courtyards and, yes, even the boundaries of Israel distinguished the set apart people of Israel and the Gentiles.

The Jordan River also serves as a boundary between wilderness and home. Across the Jordan River (Transjordan) was wild. It was rugged. It wasn't home. Home was on the west side of the Jordan. This was where the Israelites belonged. It was their land. They had a legal right to occupancy, the deed written by God. It wasn't just that east of the Jordan River was untamed and west of the Jordan River was fertile; it was the difference between wandering aimlessly and being home.

Thus the Jordan River is also the symbolic boundary between heaven and earth. The earth is good. God said so, many times (Genesis 1). The earth is given to us to enjoy. Even after we humans ruined God's perfect creation with sin, it is given back to us. It is redeemed (bought back). We are to enjoy this place and be responsible stewards of this gift, but it is not home (2 Corinthians 5:1).

No wonder, then, that Christians have seen crossing the Jordan as a metaphor for going home. We cross from this life to the next. We die but live. We go home. We cross Jordan. But in order to go home, we need to be clean. We are approaching God. We cannot enter the house dressed like this! We cannot arrive at the Lamb's high feast looking like this! We need to be holy. So God provides the clothes:

> Before the coming of this faith, we were held in custody under the law, locked up until the faith that was to come would be revealed. So the law was our guardian until Christ came that we might be justified by faith. Now that this faith has come, we are no longer under a guardian. So in Christ Jesus you are all children of God through faith, for all of you who were baptized into Christ have clothed yourselves with Christ. There is neither Jew nor Gentile, neither slave nor free, nor is there male and female, for you are all one in Christ Jesus. If you belong to Christ, then you are Abraham's seed, and heirs according to the promise. (Galatians 3:23-29)

You are set apart; that is, you are holy. You are made righteous in Christ. God provides the clothes for the heavenly banquet. It is the righteous robe of Christ. Notice the clean/unclean distinction again. We are stained with sin. There are two ways to deal with a stain: wash it or cover it. The Bible describes Baptism in both ways: a washing and a covering up of sin with the righteous robe of Christ. Notice also that the justified in faith are truly Abraham's children, Jew or Gentile. Abraham was promised this land. The deed was written by God's promise-Word. We are heirs to this estate, not the land between the Jordan and the Mediterranean but a heavenly promised land. This time the deed is written in blood and water. Our home is described in Revelation. It is the new Jerusalem, a golden Jerusalem. It is a city of gold and precious jewels (Revelation 21). It is our home.

The church employs one last picture of covering as a reminder of Baptism: the funeral pall. A white cloth is often placed over the casket of a Christian. It's a beautiful scene. How could we not recall Paul's words of being clothed in Christ when we enter a sanctuary and see a casket draped in white? It is as if God was looking down upon the deceased, deciding whether this person is worthy of heaven. And when he gazes from heaven he does not see the person and the faults or the sins, mistakes, and failures. He sees Christ. He sees righteousness. He sees one worthy of heaven and he bellows from heaven, "Well done, good and faithful servant!" You are worthy. The funeral pall is a beautiful symbol of your baptismal gown. You are clothed in Christ.

# 21

# CONTINUALLY MARKED WITH BLESSING

Jacob met his estranged brother, Esau, after crossing the Jordan River (Genesis 32,33). He finished his exile beyond the borders of the Promised Land and returned home. It was not a lighthearted journey. He had wronged his brother. He had stolen his brother's birthright and fatherly blessing. He knew there would be a reckoning. As Jacob approached his ancestral homeland, he divided his household of wives, children, and servants, thinking that if Esau attacked and killed the first wave, he would still have some of his wealth and household left. Yet something remarkable occurred. Instead of vengeance, there was a reconciliation. Instead of violence, there was love. Forgiveness. All was fine. The past was the past. Now it was different. "Welcome home, brother."

Instead of a curse, Jacob received a blessing. Is it not ironic that the thief of a blessing would be blessed? This is how God operates. Make no mistake about it, there will be a reckoning. You will be held accountable for your actions. We approach God and are deserving of a curse. But God will see Christ's righteousness instead. When we deserve curse, we receive blessing. We are reconciled with God though Christ (2 Corinthians 5:18). All is well.

Your children deserve a curse. Have they not disobeyed you? Have they not been ungrateful? You feed them. You clothe them. You protect them. You provide for them. It makes no sense that they would "bite the hand that feeds them," as the saying goes, but they do. We should stop right here and ponder that for a moment. Parents largely control their children's destiny. What would happen if you did not nourish them? What would happen to them if you did not make sure they got an education? It makes no sense whatsoever that they would ever disobey. You could also do great harm to them. You are bigger, stronger, and smarter. So why would they ever complain, disobey, or even mouth off? The answer is, they know you won't. They know you will not harm them. It is because of grace, an undeserved love. They don't bring anything to the table. Sure they bring you delight and joy, but it's not like they earn an income. It's not like they pay rent. They don't pay for their share of the electric bill or the grocery bill, let alone insurance, or chip in for the mortgage payment. But still they know that you will love them and provide for them and protect them. They are secure in your love. Their mouthing off? It is not only because of sin but also because of grace that they know you won't harm them.[5]

Your children are no different than the Israelites after the exodus. Ungrateful. Unable to deal with freedom. Complainers. So were you. So *are* you. Despite their grumbling, God blessed them. God marked them. He

---

[5]How sad to live in a household where this violence is actually a threat. Those who do live under this cloud understand even more what a parent's love is supposed to be: unconditional.

put his name on them. He told the priests to say, "The LORD bless you and keep you . . ." and with that God put his name on his children (Numbers 6:22-27). So bless your children. Literally bless them. When they go to bed at night, say, "The Lord bless you and keep you . . ." And with that you will put God's name on them. You speak for God at that moment. You are the icon of the heavenly Father when you, as a parent, bless your children. Even when they disobey, actually, *precisely* when they grumble and complain, bless them. This is love. This is grace. Turn a parental face to your children and say, "The Lord look on you with favor."

Remember that words have power. God's Word has power. God's Word has creative power. It can make dead hearts alive in faith just as it made light from nothing in the very beginning. Your words of blessing have power. Once again we are out of our modern comfort zone. The ancients knew the power of words, especially vows but blessings too. This helps us understand another curious part of the Jacob and Esau story. Jacob stole Esau's birthright. He preyed on his wild brother's impulsiveness. Esau was starving one day, and Jacob offered some soup for the birthright, to be number one in the next generation of the family estate. Esau despised his birthright and sold it. With the help of his mother, Jacob also tricked his father, Isaac, into giving him the fatherly blessing instead of Esau. Jacob pretended to be Esau at the time of this special ritual. The old man was going blind and could hear the voice of Jacob, but he smelled wild game and felt the fur of animal skin that Jacob wore pretending to be the hairy Esau. So Isaac blessed the wrong son. He blessed the younger twin and not the elder son.

Now here is the curious part. Why not take back the words? Why not say, "Oops, that was a mistake. I meant this for Esau, not Jacob. These are just words after all." But they weren't just words. Words matter. They have consequences. This blessing was not a magical spell, but neither were these words meaningless. Words matter. Your words to your children matter. So bless them. You mark your children when you bless them. A relationship is established. One of parent-child love. It is a sacred bond. It is also a Father-child relationship. The Father's relationship with his children. It is a sacred bond. A baptismal bond. A child is adopted into the family of God. And one day, reconciled in Christ, that child will be welcomed home—on the other side of Jordan.

# 22.

# THE WILDERNESS LIFE

The Israelite journey from Egypt to the Promised Land was bookended with water. The exodus was through the Red Sea and the eisodus traveled through the Jordan River. It was an exit and an entrance. It was a beginning and an end, but it was also an end and a beginning. It was the beginning of a journey that ended with a new home, but it was also the end of their slavery and the beginning of a new life of freedom. It was a water journey. It began with blood (Passover lambs) and water (Red Sea). In the middle there was water from a rock that sustained them, and it ended with a watery entrance (the Jordan River).

The Christian life mirrors their journey. The baptismal life is a watery journey. It begins with the water of Baptism and the blood of Christ. It is sustained with the living water of Christ's Word and the heavenly Bread of Life, manna from heaven, and it ends with the same watery baptismal promise in which it began: "You are a child of God, an heir to the promised land." Baptism is the beginning of a journey through life that ends in paradise. Baptism is also the end of slavery and the beginning of freedom.

If you live long enough, you will become infantile again. It is a sad outcome to life, but there is a beautiful picture amidst the darkness. You are always a child of

God. Even as you grow into adulthood, you are a child of God. Jesus praised the faith of children, especially in comparison to the jaded hubris of adults who think so highly of themselves.

> People were bringing little children to Jesus for him to place his hands on them, but the disciples rebuked them. When Jesus saw this, he was indignant. He said to them, "Let the little children come to me, and do not hinder them, for the kingdom of God belongs to such as these. Truly I tell you, anyone who will not receive the kingdom of God like a little child will never enter it." And he took the children in his arms, placed his hands on them and blessed them. (Mark 10:13-16).

Children trust better than adults. Children know they are dependent. They are not easily tricked into believing that they can do things themselves. Notice the blessing again! Jesus declares that the kingdom of God belongs to them.

Sometimes we adults, especially in a post-Enlightenment world, lose the delight of wonderment. Everything must be reduced to its simplest explanation. Love is explained by chemical interactions. Justice is measured in mandatory sentences. The cosmos is explained fully by theories that eliminate even a hint of design. We lose the wonderment of a childlike faith. Children are curious but are satisfied and even delight in the unknown, the mysterious, even the spiritual. This bothers jaded adults. We need to know. We need to know everything. I suppose it is a control thing. But do you really want a God you can understand? That is a small God.

So if you live long enough, it is a scary and often humiliating experience to grow so old that you lose your independence. But could it be a blessing? Unspoken words from God that declare you a child once again, a child to whom the kingdom of God belongs? A child who delights in the coming unknown. *What will heaven really be like? I am so close,* you might think lying in a nursing home bed. It is true, you may have to have the children you once cared for care for you to handle your minimal income and drive you to your doctor appointments. Maybe you will live in their homes rent free like they did for so many years. It may get to the point where you will need someone to feed you, bathe you, even change your diaper. If you live long enough, you may become infantile once again.

You will be right where God wants you to be. Dependent. Dependent on him. When the doctors can no longer halt death, when the government can no longer protect your life (it cannot stop death either), and when you cannot depend on yourself for your basic needs, that is when you realize, *I am a child of God.* Even though you may have the wrinkles of old age instead of the wrinkles of baby fat, you are still precious in the eyes of the Father, your Father. And your life will be bookended. It began with a watery promise of adoption, and in the end, infantile again perhaps, it will be the same promise that sustains you as you prepare to cross Jordan into the next life. The same promise-Word of Baptism.

But before you get there, you journey. It is a wilderness journey with lots of blessings but also lots of heartache. God feeds you with manna. He sustains your faith with his Word, with his body and blood, and with preaching and teaching. Israel got through its 40 years and so will you. There are oases along the way. Not mirages, but respites of grace. Heavenly food in Holy Communion that mirrors the great heavenly banquet. Words of comfort that drop from heaven before you hear Christ preach from his throne. Songs of praise that serve as choir practice for the day you will sing with the angels, "Holy, holy, holy" (Revelation 4:8), "Hallelujah" (Revelation 19:1), and "Worthy is the Lamb" (Revelation 5:12). Water, manna, and quail for Israel. Word, meal, and absolution for you. Bookended with water. The Red Sea on one side, and Jordan at the other. Baptism at both ends, and all the way through too.

# 23

# THE BEGINNING OF THE BAPTISMAL LIFE IN CHRIST

There are many honors the Bible bestows upon Jesus. He is Alpha and Omega, the beginning and the end. He is Prophet, Priest, and King. He is the Messiah, that is, the Christ. He is Key of David and Emmanuel, God with us. He is the judge and he is the Savior. He is the Son of Man and the Son of God. He is the eternal Logos who orders all things and the Lord over all. He is many things and has many names, but all of this remains distant unless he comes to us.

In Baptism we are made intimate with Christ. We die and rise with him. We suffer with him and he suffers for us. This is how Christ pulls us into himself. We are *in* Christ. He pulls us into his story and makes us a part of his story. It is our sinful nature crucified and buried at the cross, and it is Christ living in us as a new creation. He pulls us into the drama. We are intimate with him.

The baptismal life is a christological life. Our righteousness is his righteousness, and our sin becomes his sin at the cross. He then uses us to love the world. Jesus himself describes the scene of his return in which he confronts the sheep, that is, believers:

When the Son of Man comes in his glory, and all the angels with him, he will sit on his glorious throne. All the nations will be gathered before him, and he will separate the people one from another as a shepherd separates the sheep from the goats. He will put the sheep on his right and the goats on his left.

Then the King will say to those on his right, "Come, you who are blessed by my Father; take your inheritance, the kingdom prepared for you since the creation of the world. For I was hungry and you gave me something to eat, I was thirsty and you gave me something to drink, I was a stranger and you invited me in, I needed clothes and you clothed me, I was sick and you looked after me, I was in prison and you came to visit me."

Then the righteous will answer him, "Lord, when did we see you hungry and feed you, or thirsty and give you something to drink? When did we see you a stranger and invite you in, or needing clothes and clothe you? When did we see you sick or in prison and go to visit you?"

The King will reply, "Truly I tell you, whatever you did for one of the least of these brothers and sisters of mine, you did for me." (Matthew 25:31-40)

Whenever the baptized serve their neighbors, they serve Christ. Neighbors are "Christ" to them. The opposite is true as well. When we are served, it is Christ serving us through these other people in their callings, or vocations. It is Christ who serves us. Christ to them and Christ to us. This baptismal life is a christological life.

The baptized need never wonder, *Where is God?* He is everywhere, and not just in his omnipresence. He is intimate. He is the one teaching our children and diagnosing our illnesses. He is the one filling potholes and constructing houses. He uses people. The ordinary for the extraordinary. The baptized have deep meaning in their lives, for they are the ones God uses to carry out these tasks for others. All in Christ. He is never far.

The baptized are honored by God. Baptism chooses a human. Baptism chooses a human to be a part of the family—to be saved, to be loved and adored by God above. Baptism also chooses these very same humans to be useful. To be a part of God's love in the world. To work with him for the good of humankind both physically and spiritually. It is the baptized who preach and teach; they are priests of God. But it is also the baptized who build roads, write laws, inspect bridges, plow fields, bring joy through art, and drive trucks—all as masks of God. In these callings they will suffer; the sign of the cross at Baptism has a dual meaning—more on that later. They suffer with Christ, for they are doing his work with him as his coworkers in the world. But this is old hat. As they die to themselves and live for others, they are only playing out the original baptismal death and resurrection. This is the baptismal life, a life of death and resurrection but also a life of great joy as they work in love until one day they enter the promised land, their inheritance guaranteed by their adoption into God's family.

There are similarities between the human condition before Baptism and the plight of the Israelites in Egypt. Remember that Israel was trapped. As mentioned before, they left Egypt without a clear pathway to the Promised Land. The Mediterranean Sea, the Red Sea, the Egyptian army, the Philistine army, and the terrain south of Egypt all made their journey seem impossible. They needed a miracle. They needed a water miracle, and they got one. This seemed to be planned by God. They needed a lesson, a lesson they had a hard time learning. They needed to trust God, and the only way to trust God is to be abundantly clear that trust in anything else is futile. The opposite of faith is actually not unbelief. Everybody believes in something or someone. Even an atheist believes in something, namely, that there is no god. More than that, we all have a number one. We all put our faith is some philosophy, person, political party, government, or theory. The opposite of faith in Christ is faith in anything else, and that usually is ourselves. So God trapped Israel.

You were born trapped. Not only were you helpless for your daily needs, but you were already set on a path toward death. It sounds so dark, but it is true: The day you are born is the first day in your journey to death. The clock starts ticking the moment of your birth, really, your conception. The clock was ticking on Israel. Egyptian charioteers were already dispatched. The Israelites needed a miracle and fast. They needed a water miracle.

The devil's charioteers were dispatched after you the first day of your life. You too have an enemy. The clock is ticking. You are trapped because of sin. You were conceived in sin (Psalm 51:5). Again, it seems so negative to think of a newborn as sinful, but what else would a child of two sinful humans be? The Bible is clear about the reality of the situation: We have original sin. Our experience only confirms this sad state of affairs. If we were born with clean slates, don't you think at least some would make it into adulthood without sin? We can't make it very far without this sinful reality rearing its ugly head. I didn't teach my children how to lie, nor did Sesame Street. They figured it out themselves.

So we are trapped in sin. So we have an enemy. So we are in a processional of death. The clock is ticking. We need a miracle. We need a water miracle and we get one. It is quite a scene to see a person paraded to the font to be baptized or to see parents march their kids to the font to receive this heavenly bath. It is a parade. It is a processional, but it is a processional of death. They carry someone dead in sin.[6] They march in death to a font of life. Something has to give.

I cannot help thinking about another procession of death when I witness parents bringing their children to Baptism. It is the funeral procession of the son of the widow of Nain (Luke 7:11-17). There are actually two processions in this story. The first begins with the casket of the dead boy. The emotions were raw that day. Jewish burials were conducted the same day as the death, before sunset. No time to mourn privately. It was not a private society anyway (privacy is a modern Western

---

[6]It should be noted that God comes in different ways to deliver salvation. Baptism is one, but so is the Word of God (Baptism is only efficacious because of the Word attached to it). Preaching can reach infant ears, and the Holy Spirit can create faith in any heart. Certainly the Spirit has and can create faith in infants before they are baptized, but the act of Baptism also creates faith.

concept). You mourned together and you did it out loud. The whole town was there. The whole town would process outside the city gate to bury *their* dead. Add to this the double tragedy of a young man/boy cut down in the prime of his life and the fact that he was the only son of a widow, all she had left, and, well, it must have been an emotional scene.

The other procession was not one of death but one of life. We are told that Jesus and his followers were parading to Nain. As they approached the city gate, they met the procession of death. Something had to give. Who would go through the gate first? Who had the right-of-way? The answer is obvious. The funeral procession should go first. It's the right thing to do. Even in our contemporary world there is still some sense of respect for the dead and their mourners. A funeral procession of cars is allowed the right-of-way. Most people still pull their vehicle over to the side of the road. It's the right thing to do.

But not that day. The procession of life would interrupt the procession of death. People were no doubt aghast at this rudeness. Jesus, the leader of this parade of life, does the unthinkable. He approaches the stretcher on which lays the dead boy, and he touches it. That would be out of line in any culture, but even more so in first-century Palestine. Remember the Old Testament laws about being in contact with dead bodies. It made one unclean. To purposefully touch a coffin was insane. Why would anybody purposefully make himself unclean, let alone offend the mourners?

Jesus would and did. His procession of life would end the procession of death. When he touched the coffin and commanded, "Young man, I say to you, get up!" (Luke 7:14), the boy was raised from the dead. The offense that day was not that Jesus didn't follow protocol; the offense was that death could have this boy. Jesus was having none of it. It was not that the uncleanness of the death would be transferred to Jesus but that the cleanness of Jesus (righteousness) was transferred to the boy. Jesus gave the boy back to his mother alive. The procession of life ended the procession of death.

This was the exact same scene at your baptism, especially if you were baptized as a child. Two processions collided at the font, one of death and one of life. Who has the right-of-way? Who will win? Who will back down? You know the answer. And the pastor, acting in the stead of Christ, hands the baby back to Mom and Dad. "Do not cry, your child will live."

# 24

# MARKED AS ONE REDEEMED BY CHRIST

Most baptisms in the history of the church have included the sign of the cross. It is not a necessary custom but a thoughtful and instructive one. Before the actual baptism, the minister says, "Receive the sign of the holy cross on your forehead and on your heart to mark you as one redeemed by Christ crucified." This act connects Baptism to the cross just as Saint Paul does in Romans chapter 6. It also marks the child as belonging to God. The child is tattooed, as it were, with the sign of the cross. Everywhere this soul travels, the devil and his minions and God and his angels will know: this one belongs to God.

From then on, that child of God, whenever she sees the sign of the cross traced by a pastor or when she herself makes the sign of the cross, she is reminded that she is redeemed by Christ crucified. It is a mobile baptismal certificate. The sign of the cross forever becomes a reminder of Baptism. This is why countless Christians for centuries have employed the sign of the cross, tracing this sacred symbol from their heads, through their hearts, and to the belt. It is an invisible shield permanently traced on their bodies and seen by the spiritual world. You can't touch this one, Satan; this one belongs to God.

The sign of the cross has then typically been made in church, at prayer, when a Christian hears of a death, or when a Christian is in danger or needs a reminder of God's grace. It, of course, can become superstitious, but only if we let it. In his Small Catechism Luther recommended making the sign of the cross when praying in the morning and the evening.[7] Again, it is not a necessary thing but a thoughtful and instructive custom. Even if you do not employ this sign on yourself, you can still remember your baptism when the preacher begins a church service in the name of the Father and of the Son and of the Holy Spirit while making the sign of the cross. It is that name in which you were baptized, and in it is that name in which you have the right to enter into the presence of God without fear on Sunday morning. You have a different relationship with the omniscient, omnipresent, and omnipotent God. He is your Father. This almighty God is on your side. You have the right to cry, "Abba, Father." Notice that the same preacher blesses you on the way out with the sign of the cross again. The threefold Aaronic blessing is trinitarian. The name of God is put on you (Numbers 6:22-27). It is also a baptismal reminder. All will be well as you go into that scary world. You are baptized. The name of God is on you. The triune God is on your side. You are redeemed by Christ crucified. Never forget it.

However, the sign of the cross at Baptism has a dual meaning. First, it reminds all who are there that this child (or adult) has been bought back (redeemed) from the

---

[7]Small Catechism, Morning and Evening Prayers, Kolb-Wengert, pp. 363,364.

clutch of Satan and now belongs to God. Christ's crucifixion paid the price for this soul. Second, the sign of the cross eerily predicts a life of the cross. This child will also suffer. Jesus promised that too: "If the world hates you, keep in mind that it hated me first. If you belonged to the world, it would love you as its own. As it is, you do not belong to the world, but I have chosen you out of the world. That is why the world hates you" (John 15:18,19).

Jesus even commands the cross: "Whoever does not take up their cross and follow me is not worthy of me" (Matthew 10:38). We should note that crosses are not chosen, but they are laid before us. A cross is any type of suffering that leads us to doubt God's love. It makes us wonder. It makes us think, *Is God really on my side?* It finally drives us to Christ. We have nowhere else to go. Our cross leads us to his cross.

It is true that we cannot know the will of God unless he gives us this insight in his Word. However, while we cannot say that a particular suffering is because of a particular cause, we are given a few reasons for suffering. Sufferings strengthen Christians (Hebrews 12:7), sufferings teach compassion for others (Philippians 2:1-11), sufferings (specifically crosses) are a mark of the church (Psalm 116:10), and sufferings drive us to repentance, which, by the grace of God, hopefully leads us to the Scriptures and ultimately to faith (Proverbs 3:5). If for no other reason, God allows (and even sends) sufferings so that we do not trust ourselves but, rather, are driven to his cross.

This is quite a burden to put on an infant, but it is truth. It is a heavy sign, the sign of the cross on the forehead and on the heart. But the yoke is light. Jesus calls for us, "Come to me, all you who are weary and burdened, and I will give you rest. Take my yoke upon you and learn from me, for I am gentle and humble in heart, and you will find rest for your souls. For my yoke is easy and my burden is light" (Matthew 11:28-30).

He is fatherly in his words here. Parents know that they send out their children into a crazy and difficult world, but they do so with confidence, reluctant as they may be. It will be all right even though their knees may be skinned, their hearts broken, or their egos bruised.

Peter actually takes it a step further, declaring that we participate in Christ's sufferings. "But rejoice inasmuch as you participate in the sufferings of Christ, so that you may be overjoyed when his glory is revealed" (1 Peter 4:13). This does not mean that Christians participate in the saving actions of the cross—not at all. Rather, as God's masks, Christians go out into the world with his love. And love will mean suffering in a broken world. If we do God's work, then we should expect suffering.

The baptismal life is a vocational life. God does not only honor us with his saving action, but he honors us with work. Saint Paul puts the two together in his letter to the Ephesians: "It is by grace you have been saved, through faith—and this is not from yourselves, it is the gift of God—not by works, so that no one can boast. For we are God's handiwork, created in Christ Jesus to do good works, which God prepared in advance for us to do" (Ephesians 2:8-10).

That child at the font is being saved by grace alone but is also being tasked with good deeds he or she cannot even comprehend yet. The sign of the cross has a dual meaning. It marks one as redeemed by Christ crucified and marks one as a coworker with God in the world. A coworker who shares in the suffering.

# 25.

# THE ARK OF THE CHURCH

Many churches place their font at the entrance to the sanctuary. It makes sense. For many Christians, this was their initiation into the church. They have entered into the family. They are adopted. It's official. From that day forward the baptized are reminded that they belong. Each and every time they enter that church (or any church where the font stands majestic at the entrance), they are reminded of their welcoming into the holy Christian church, their forgiveness in Christ, their adoption into God's family, and their inheritance of heaven.

It works on the way out too. The psalmist promised that "the Lord will keep you from all harm—he will watch over your life; the Lord will watch over your coming and going both now and forevermore" (Psalm 121:7,8). As you enter and as you leave, you are reminded of God's promise-Word to watch over you. He made a promise to protect you from sin, death, and this world. You are his dear child. You enter with a baptismal reminder: "I belong here, this is my Father I approach today." And you leave with promises of God: "He will watch over my coming and going."

We mentioned that the invocation at the beginning of the service has baptismal overtones. It is in this triune name in which we are baptized, and it is this same tri-une God whose name we invoke at the beginning of the service. We have a different relationship with the Almighty, one of family. He is our Father. At the end of the service there is typically a threefold blessing as well, usually the same words God commanded Aaron to place upon the Israelites so as to put his name on them. We can also recall the promises Jesus left his disciples before he ascended into heaven.

During Jesus' passion and at his ascension he made five promises we might call ascension promises. There are more, of course, but these five constitute a package of promises he left with his disciples and, by extension, us as we leave the presence of God on Sunday into the same crazy world in which the apostles ventured. I will always be with you to the very end of the age (Matthew 28:20). I will send you the Spirit (John 14:25-27). I will prepare a place for you (John 14:1). I will rule all things for your benefit (Matthew 26:64). Finally, I will come back for you (John 14:28; Acts 1:11). When we leave church with this blessing and pass by the font one last time, we are com-forted that Christ will fulfill his promise to us. He hasn't let us down yet.

Many church buildings resemble a boat. This also makes sense. If you look up into the ceiling of many churches, it looks like the hull of a ship. This is mean-ingful because the church is like a ship. In this ship you are safe from the roaring seas of this world. The ancients feared the sea for the most part. So should we. It is a dan-gerous place. The ancients spun all sorts of tales about the seas, stories that were mystical, even spiritual. While these stories are only myths, they point to a greater reality that we live in a spiritual realm. It's dangerous out there. It's spiritually dangerous out there.

Noah was safe in the ark. The disciples were safe in a boat when Jesus calmed the winds and the waves of the Sea of Galilee. Fishers of men bring souls (fish) into the ship by the net of the gospel. These vessels may be tossed and turned, but this ship of the church is the safest place there is. This does not mean there will not be trouble in this world, nor does it mean there will not be trouble inside the ship—there will be. But to be in the boat means that you are a member of the church, that is, the spiritual body of Christ, all believers everywhere of all time. Despite the world's winds and waves, despite attempted mutinies on the boat, you are safe—eternally safe.

Speaking of Noah's ark, did you know that many baptismal fonts have eight sides? Once again we see the wisdom of the church that teaches us. Peter connected the flood with Baptism:

> Christ also suffered once for sins, the righteous for the unrighteous, to bring you to God. He was put to death in the body but made alive in the Spirit. After being made alive, he went and made proclamation to the imprisoned spirits—to those who were disobedient long ago when God waited patiently in the days of Noah while the ark was being built. In it only a few people, eight in all, were saved through water, and this water symbolizes baptism that now saves you also—not the removal of dirt from the body but the pledge of a clear conscience toward God. It saves you by

the resurrection of Jesus Christ, who has gone into heaven and is at God's right hand—with angels, authorities and powers in submission to him. (1 Peter 3:18-22)

Peter was speaking about Christian suffering in this section of his letter, but notice that he connected it to Baptism and the resurrection (we are crucified and resurrected with our Lord)—it is finally Christ's actions that save. Peter also mentioned the flood in Noah's day. Noah suffered, as will baptized Christians, but Noah was saved by water, as are baptized Christians. Peter makes a point, albeit not the main point, of telling us that eight people were in the ark: Noah and his wife, their three sons, and their wives. This is why many fonts have eight sides. It is the artist's subtle way of pointing us to the flood-baptism connection.

The number 8 is used in Scripture a few times. Eight people in the ark, Israelite boys were circumcised on the eighth day, and Jesus rose on the eighth day. Since then eight has become a symbol of eternity, resurrection, and new beginning. If 7 is the number of completion (God created and rested during the first seven-day week), so 8 is the elusive eternal day. To this day we still employ a seven-day week. The problem is that there is always a Monday! We repeat the cycle over and over. The battle between the old man and the new creation keeps repeating—death and resurrection, sin and grace, old and new—until one day we enter an eternal rest after our six days of labor here on earth. "There remains, then, a Sabbath-rest for the people of God" (Hebrews 4:9). The seventh day of rest reaches into eternity, the elusive eighth day. No wonder Jesus rose on Sunday, the first and the eighth day of the week. No wonder baptismal fonts often have eight sides.

Baptism is a new beginning and promises us the eternal Sabbath rest. Baptism is even spoken of as a rebirth. Jesus declared that we must be born again. Nicodemus, Jesus' singular audience one evening, was incredulous at Jesus' assertion that a man must be born again. " 'How can someone be born when they are old?' Nicodemus asked. 'Surely they cannot enter a second time into their mother's womb to be born!' " (John 3:4). Christ offered a water answer: "Very truly I tell you, no one can enter the kingdom of God unless they are born of water and the Spirit. Flesh gives birth to flesh, but the Spirit gives birth to spirit" (John 3:5,6).

Another connection with the church and Baptism has to do with motherhood. Newborns need mothers. We often miss this picture in the church. It is vague, to be sure, and no doubt controversial, but we shouldn't ignore it. The church acts like a mother. Paul hints at this in Galatians chapter 4. Paul is comparing Hagar and Sarah to freedom and slavery. His connection of the church to motherhood is not the main point, but still it lingers: "Now Hagar stands for Mount Sinai in Arabia and corresponds to the present city of Jerusalem, because she is in slavery with her children. But the Jerusalem that is above is free, and she is our mother" (Galatians 4:25,26).

The new Jerusalem is the kingdom of God. It is heaven. It is all believers. It is the church—not a denomination but the holy Christian church, the spiritual body of Christ. And it is like a mother. Mothers give life and nurture, and that is exactly what the church does.

Certainly it is God who gives life, through both the natural order of birth and the new life in Christ (dead to sin, alive in him). Notice, however, that he uses women in particular to carry out the grand task of giving birth to human beings. It is quite an honor. We see God's *modus operandi* again, using the ordinary to accomplish the extraordinary. So it is when he rebirths. It is through mother church. He uses ordinary means once again. She baptizes. She teaches. She nurtures. She gathers the chicks as a hen. She worries. She protects. She serves. She welcomes back prodigal children like only a mother can. She provides a home. She fills the home with song and decoration. She sends out children into the world. No, Nicodemus, you cannot re-enter your mother's womb, but you do emerge reborn from the preaching of the gospel. Baptized and born again, from the womb of the font. No longer dead in sin but reborn into life. This life comes from God through the church, and then God uses the church to nurture and care for the reborn in Baptism.

# 26

# A RIVER FLOWS FROM CHRIST

The Garden of Eden was off-limits to Adam and Eve after their rebellion. They lost the righteousness of God, but God promised his righteousness to them through his Son, their son, the Messiah. Angels guarded the entrance to their original paradise, but angels would sing as they entered another paradise. Eden would be restored. This new Eden too has a river, and it flows from Christ. But before we get all the way to the last chapter of the Bible, the one that describes a river flowing from the throne of the Lamb, we hear about God's presence with his people before they, like John the evangelist, are shown the river of life.

As we have seen, God is everywhere but chooses to be in specific places so that his people know where he can be found in grace. Nature only tells about God's might; his gospel tells us of his love. He set up a home for himself, the tabernacle and, later, the temple. There he would be with his people. They could come into his presence without fear because of the coming sacrifice that would pay for their ungodly rebellion.

The temple played a role in the vision given to Ezekiel (Ezekiel 47). A man showed Jerusalem, specifically the temple, to Ezekiel. It was a foreshadowing of the return of the Jewish exiles from Babylon but, ultimately, of a new Jerusalem, a new Israel, and a new creation. It was a vision of heaven. After touring the temple and inspecting all of its architecture, Ezekiel saw the priests working and the glory of God shining. The vision zooms out for a moment to the land of Israel, the Promised Land, and then back to the east side of Jerusalem, where the temple butts up to the edge of Jerusalem overlooking a valley.

Ezekiel saw the headwaters of a river, a different kind of river. The water came from the temple and eventually emptied into the Dead Sea. This special river not only allowed for plants to flourish on its banks but even turned the Dead Sea, full of salt, into fresh water. Fish were so aplenty that fishermen stood on the shore of the Dead Sea with their nets for great catches. Fruit trees around the formerly dead area produced fruit every month. If you were listening to Ezekiel preach this vision, you would have been astounded at the contrast between the arid and dead area turning to life, let alone the description of a temple that had been destroyed by Babylon, Israel's enemy.

John too had a vision of a river and fruit trees bearing fruit every month. His vision was of Christ on his throne. Jesus is described as the Lamb so that we never forget the grace of the cross. Christ, who is symbolized by the altar and the temple, is in the center of the new Jerusalem, a restored Eden, and its river flows from his altar as in Ezekiel's vision. This was always the case. It was always the pre-incarnate Christ and his presence among the people. It is always Christ whose life-giving words, healing body and blood, forgiving absolution, and watery baptism are at the center of our lives. Here is what John saw:

Then the angel showed me the river of the water of life, as clear as crystal, flowing from the throne of God and of the Lamb down the middle of the great street of the city. On each side of the river stood the tree of life, bearing twelve crops of fruit, yielding its fruit every month. And the leaves of the tree are for the healing of the nations. No longer will there be any curse. The throne of God and of the Lamb will be in the city, and his servants will serve him. They will see his face, and his name will be on their foreheads. There will be no more night. They will not need the light of a lamp or the light of the sun, for the Lord God will give them light. And they will reign for ever and ever. (Revelation 22:1-5)

This is a fitting ending to Scripture: Eden restored, thirst quenched, peace among the nations. The angel points Adam and Eve, and we their sinful descendants, to the tree and the river. Adam and Eve (and we their descendants), who once were banned by angels, are welcomed home. All of us prodigal children.

The original audiences of Ezekiel and John were simi-lar. Both were threatened by large economic and military powers (Babylon and Rome, respectively). Oppressed. Seemingly without hope or even a home. All they had was the future. You may not live under oppression like the exiles of Israel or the early church under the pall of Roman oppression, but you are not yet home. So why hope? Because God has gotten his people through worse. He has never let us down. The baptized have been given a promise, a promise-Word, and God keeps his word. You know where you are going and you know what it looks like. You have been guaranteed water, something you cannot always count on in this world. Not just access to a stream or a spring that runs through your faucet, but a living, giving water that quenches all thirst. Eden is restored and Eden is for the baptized.

# 27

# THE FATHER'S ETERNAL LOVE

When we began to follow the red line of watery imagery through the Scriptures, we started with creation. We noticed that words matter. They have power. God's words have creative power. Just as the Spirit hovered (or fluttered) over the waters, so the Spirit was active in your baptism. Just as all things were created through the Son, so your baptism was a baptism into Christ's death and resurrection. Just as God said, "Let there be light," and there was light, so God said, "Let there be faith," and there was faith. A living faith in a dead heart. God's words have creative power at the beginning and at your baptism. After acknowledging the similarities between the creation of the world and the creation of your faith, we dared to say that both were of equal importance. That might sound like hyperbole, but this is how God operates. He is both beyond us and intimate with us. The Creator cares about his creation. The one who magnificently created all animals knows when a single sparrow falls to the ground. The one who holds all things in his hand knows how many hairs are on your head.

The Father-child imagery is of great comfort. Even if you did not have a good father or didn't have a father at all, you know (maybe more than most) what a good father is supposed to be. A father is supposed to be a paradox. He is supposed to be powerful but gentle. He is supposed to be feared but loved. He is the one who one moment stands between danger and his child and in the next moment reads a book to a toddler. A father is one who speaks boldly but tenderly. He is the one whose toughness is tough for a reason: his child. Now listen to the Father's words to his baptized children:

> Those God foreknew he also predestined to be conformed to the image of his Son, that he might be the firstborn among many brothers and sisters. And those he predestined, he also called; those he called, he also justified; those he justified, he also glorified. What, then, shall we say in response to these things? If God is for us, who can be against us? He who did not spare his own Son, but gave him up for us all—how will he not also, along with him, graciously give us all things? (Romans 8:29-32)

Through Saint Paul the Father says to you, "Don't you know, little child, that before the beginning of time I knew you? I knew you and I loved you. In fact, all of this is for you." Imagine a father leaning over the rail of his newborn's crib and barely audibly saying, "I will never, ever let anything happen to you. I would gladly lay down my life for you. I will give you everything you need and probably a lot more if you ask! It is as if you were always a part of me—that I was meant to be your father, that from all eternity this was meant to be."

The Father in heaven made a promise. He gave you his word and he always keeps his word. He always knew you and loved you. He predestined you for the heavenly estate. This is your family inheritance. So he made sure that you, whom he predestined, would be called by the Holy Spirit to believe. He made sure that you, whom he called, would be justified in the blood of Christ. He made sure that you, whom he justified, would be glorified in all eternity. He made a baptismal promise to you, his child. His promises have power because his Word has power. His Word has creative power. He created this universe and all that exists with his Word. That same Word, with that same power, backs up his promise to you. "I always knew you. I knew you and I loved you."

# 28.

# CONCLUSION

Holy Scripture is dripping wet. From the beginning the Spirit fluttered over water as God's creative Word made something from nothing. "Let there be light," and there was light. His words have power, creative power. His gracious Word is a promise-Word and he always keeps his word. He promised a Savior for rebellious sinners. He kept that promise alive when he pushed up the ark high above destroying waters to keep Noah and his family and, with them, the line of the Savior alive.

He reminded his people of this promise by marking them in circumcision and placing his name on them. He taught them that this was a washing away of sins by catechizing them through ceremonial washing rituals. He escaped Israel from Egyptian slavery through a water miracle in the Red Sea. He quenched the Israelites' thirst with water from a rock as he fed them with manna and quail. He crossed them over the Jordan River into a promised land. He sprinkled them with blood and washed away Naaman's disease.

Then he sent his Son to make these pictures reality. He offered up his firstborn, the price for freedom, first symbolically at the temple and then on the altar of the cross. He circumcised his Son, the first drop of blood shed for our salvation, as Jesus fulfilled the law in our place. Christ dipped himself into the Jordan River, sanctifying the Jordan and all waters of Baptism as a washing away of sins. He went into the wilderness to be tempted just as Israel was, but this time without failure. He does what we could not do.

Then he commanded this Baptism for all so that he could die and rise with his people in a most intimate way. He marks them as ones redeemed by Christ crucified and then honors them with work. He places them in the church to be nurtured, loved, and adored. He circumcises their hearts and continually kills and raises the new creation. He pulls them into his life, into him. He is intimate, never far, always there. He looks over their coming and their going. He gives confidence to the baptized: "Bring it on, world! You can't take away my baptism." He leaps off the dripping wet pages of Scripture and into the hands of a lowly preacher and declares, "I baptize you."

So when the time is right for you, when all is done, when there is no more to say and no more to accomplish, when death knocks at the door, when it comes time to cross Jordan to receive your inheritance, hold on to the watery promise. Clutch your baptismal certificate. It is your legal deed to the promised land. Don't worry, even if you don't have that piece of paper; it is okay, your name has already been written permanently in the book of life (Philippians 4:3). You will hear, as you cross Jordan, the same voice that bellowed above the real Jordan when John baptized Jesus: "This is my son. This is my daughter. With them I am well pleased." And the Spirit will flutter as always over the water.

# ADDENDUM: COMMENTARY ON THE BAPTISM ORDER

Baptism at its core is a promise-Word attached to water that delivers salvation. It is at once majestic and simple, powerful and meek. God's creative Word brings life from death, shines light in darkness, and changes sinful hearts into righteous hearts. It is power. It is also ordinary water. It is not gold or silver that God uses but the fundamental element of his creation. It is both beyond us and accessible. This is how God operates.

It is fitting, then, that the baptismal formula is simple. All you need is water and these words: "I baptize you in the name of the Father and of the Son and of the Holy Spirit." God does the rest. Any Christian can perform this divine rite. Yet Christians have added rituals to this rite that are instructive, symbolic, and even beautiful. A marriage rite is simple: "Do you take Lucy to be your wife? Do you take Tom to be your husband? I pronounce you husband and wife." That's really all there is. But we know that marriage is a profound gift from God, so we add prayers and songs, symbolic rituals, and even a banquet in order to lift our gaze to the heavenly banquet of the Lamb (Revelation 19:9) and to the holy estate of marriage. So it is with Baptism.

What follows is a rite that Martin Luther added to the end of his Small Catechism. It is not entirely his but was handed down to him throughout the generations. Luther modified it here and there with some beautiful additions, most notably, the "flood prayer."[8] I too have updated language. In the end it is the church's rite. It is neither right nor wrong. I only use it here to bring out some of the beautiful realties of God's grace in Baptism. So a baptism might begin like this:

*Pastor: Peace be with you.*
*Congregation: And with your spirit.*

Peace is a good way to begin this rite. We are at peace with God. We shouldn't be. We have been prodigal. More than that, we are born enemies of God. Rebels, the worst kind, ones without a moral cause. But we say, "Peace." We have been reconciled with God through Christ. All is well between us and the Lawgiver. We are righteous. So why should there be animosity between us sinners? Christ who is the Prince of peace has brought us peace. We employ many greetings in our world. "Good morning!" "How are you?" But these will not do for this special occasion. "Peace" is deeper and more meaningful than trite words. Peace means that we are reconciled to God and one another, and that results in a robust and full life here on earth with our friends, families, and neighbors.

*Pastor: What do you seek?*
*Candidate: The Sacrament of Holy Baptism.*

---

[8]For Luther's historic text of the Baptism Order, see Kolb-Wengert, pp. 371-375. See also *Luther's Works*, Vol. 53, pp. 107-109.

Now we get to business. We are here for a washing. This is not a forced baptism, as if pastors are to spray water on pedestrians walking on the sidewalk. So the pastor asks, "What do you want? What are you here for? Does everybody understand what this is about?" This begs the question, How can a child, let alone a mere infant, desire this? How can the child answer when he or she cannot speak? And are we not told that the dead in sin cannot make themselves alive? So how can any sinner, child or adult, answer with anything other than "No!" More on this later, but for now we will say that whatever God demands of us, he provides for us in Christ. He provides the faith and faith confesses. So the sponsors (godparents) or parents speak for those who cannot speak (a child).

*Pastor: What is your name?*
*Candidate: [Name].*

Along these same lines, the pastor asks the child's name. This is an official act. In most cases it will be recorded. A certificate will be filled out and given to the family. This is personal but also public. The candidate stands before the almighty God to be counted. On these occasions many Christians in the history of the church received their names as well.

*Pastor: Depart, unclean spirit! Give way to the Holy Spirit!*

This line sounds strange to our modern ears. Its title, "exorcism," sounds even weirder. Exorcisms are for horror movies or superstitious eras of the past, right? Not so fast. Once we get past the name and think about the theology of this, we understand how deeply moving this line is. This command to the devil and prayer to the Holy Spirit is nothing more than what Saint Paul laid out in his letter to the Roman congregation. Either a person is a slave to sin or a slave to righteousness. Either you are dead or you are alive (Romans 6:15-18). While Paul contrasts the flesh with the Spirit (flesh equaling the sinful nature and the Spirit equaling the new person living in us through the Holy Spirit), both are spiritual. He is not declaring the body bad and the spiritual good. Both are sinful and both are redeemed in Christ. Either you are spiritually sinful (and bodily too) or you are declared righteous, both body and spirit. You are either believer or unbeliever. Either you are of God or you are of this sinful world and the prince of this world, the devil, no matter how outwardly pious you might be. Paul said,

> You, however, are not in the realm of the flesh but are in the realm of the Spirit, if indeed the Spirit of God lives in you. And if anyone does not have the Spirit of Christ, they do not belong to Christ. (Romans 8:9)

So depart, unclean spirit, and give way to the Holy Spirit!

*[Name], receive the sign of the holy cross on your forehead and on your heart to mark you as one redeemed by Christ crucified.*

The cross is never far from a Christian's heart and mind. As we have already said, the cross and Baptism are connected, or better yet, Baptism connects a Christian with the cross in a most intimate way (Romans 6).

The baptized are marked with this sign that they can employ throughout their lives to be reminded that they are redeemed by Christ crucified, that they are protected by God, and that they will bear a cross with Christ in their Christian life of love.

*Pastor: Let us pray.*

*O almighty and eternal God, the Father of Our Lord Jesus Christ: I call to you for the sake of your servant, [Name], who asks for the gift of your Baptism and desires your eternal grace through spiritual rebirth. Receive him/her, Lord, and as you have said, "Ask, and it will be given to you; seek, and you will find; knock, and it will be opened to you," so now give the blessing to him/her who asks and open the door to him/her who knocks so that he/she may obtain the eternal blessing of this heavenly bath and receive the promised kingdom of your grace; through Jesus Christ our Lord. Amen.*

*Almighty and eternal God, who according to your righteous judgment condemned the unbelieving world through the flood, and in your great mercy preserved believing Noah and his family, who drowned hard-hearted Pharaoh with all his host in the Red Sea and led your people Israel through the same on dry ground thereby prefiguring this bath of your Holy Baptism, and who through the baptism of your beloved Son, our Lord Jesus Christ, sanctified and set apart the Jordan and all water as a blessed flood and a rich and full washing away of sins: according to the same boundless mercy, we pray that you graciously behold [Name] and bless him/her with true faith in the Spirit so that, by means of this saving flood, all that has been born in him/her from Adam and which he himself/she herself has added to may be drowned in him/her and engulfed; and that he/she may be saved from the number of unbelieving, preserved dry and secure in the holy ark of Christendom, serve your name at all times fervent in spirit and joyful in hope; so that with all believers he/she may be made worthy to attain eternal life according to your promise; through Jesus Christ, your Son, our Lord, who lives and reigns with you and the Holy Spirit, one God, now and forever. Amen.*

These prayers passionately capture the power of Baptism seen through the lens of both the Old and New Testaments. The doctrines of original sin and grace in Christ are present. So are the Old Testament pictures of the flood and Red Sea. A connection to Christ, specifically his baptism in the Jordan River, is made. Finally, and this is what prayer is finally about, we ask God to do what he promised. We hold forth his promises in his presence and say, "You promised! This is all we have. We come before you with nothing else. We take you at your word." So give this good (salvation through Baptism) to he who asks and open the door to she who knocks.

*Pastor: Hear now the holy Gospel according to Saint Mark.*

*They brought little children to Jesus, that he might touch them; but the disciples rebuked those who brought them. But when Jesus saw it, he was greatly displeased and said to them, "Let the little children come to me, and do not forbid them; for such is the kingdom of God. Assuredly, I say to you, whoever does not receive the kingdom of God as a little child will by no means enter it." And he took them up in his arms, put his hands on them, and blessed them.*

*Pastor: The Gospel of the Lord.*
*Congregation: Thanks be to God.*

This gospel reading is a wonderful teaching tool about both faith and Baptism. We are always little children no matter how old we are. In fact, Jesus says that unless we believe in the trustworthy manner of children, we don't belong in his kingdom. We are completely dependent on him for our salvation, like a child is of his or her parents. One way to remind ourselves of this dependence, which also serves as our confidence, is to frame and hang our baptismal certificates on our bedroom wall. No matter what comes our way that day, our adoption into God's family cannot be taken away. It is a fact of history that has already occurred.

*Congregation: Our Father who art in heaven. Hallowed be thy name. Thy kingdom come. Thy will be done on earth as it is in heaven. Give us this day our daily bread. And forgive us our trespasses, as we forgive those who trespass against us. And lead us not into temptation. But deliver us from evil. For thine is the kingdom and the power and the glory forever and ever. Amen.*

The Lord's Prayer is the most perfect prayer since it came from our Savior's lips, but it is also the perfect prayer for Baptism. Think of the first two words: "Our Father." They are the sweetest and the most difficult words of the prayer. They are the most difficult because starting a prayer is often the most difficult aspect of prayer. They are the sweetest because they are pure gospel: "Father." "Father" means that we have a relationship of love with God. All the adjectives the Bible uses to describe God (all-powerful, all-knowing, etc.) are fearful attributes. But if the relationship is father and child, then an encounter with the Almighty is not frightening but comforting. He is on my side. God is still to be feared, but in the proper sense. There is a lot to the word *Father.* And the relationship is solidified in the adoption of Baptism. "Our Father" is a baptismal address.

> Pastor: *[Name], do you renounce the devil?*
> Candidate: *I do renounce.*
>
> Pastor: *Do you renounce all his works?*
> Candidate: *I do renounce.*
>
> Pastor: *Do you renounce all his ways?*
> Candidate: *I do renounce.*

The renunciations once again display the seriousness of the situation. We are people between God and the devil. This is how valuable we are to both: A cosmic battle has been fought and is still raging between God and Satan. The prize is you. Christians live in the already/not yet. The battle has *already* been won, but it is *not yet* over. We are *already* heirs of the kingdom but have *not yet* reaped its full rewards. The renunciations remind us of this battle, our importance, and that it is an either/or matter. Either we are of God or of the devil. "Whoever is not with me is against me, and whoever does not gather with me scatters" (Matthew 12:30). So do you renounce the devil and all his works and all his ways?

*Pastor: Do you believe in God the Father almighty, maker of heaven and earth?*
*Candidate: I do believe.*

*Pastor: Do you believe in Jesus Christ, his only Son, our Lord, who was conceived by the Holy Spirit, born of the virgin Mary, suffered under Pontius Pilate, was crucified, died, and was buried. He descended into hell. On the third day he rose again from the dead. He ascended into heaven and is seated at the right hand of God the Father almighty. From there he will come to judge the living and the dead?*
*Candidate: I do believe.*

*Pastor: Do you believe in the Holy Spirit, the holy Christian church, the communion of saints, the forgiveness of sins, the resurrection of the body, and the life everlasting?*
*Candidate: I do believe.*

The other side of the coin from the renunciations of the devil is a confession of the truth of God. So the candidate is asked if he or she believes in the triune God. But how can a child believe and assent to this faith, let alone articulate this faith? We maintain the following:

1. Life begins at conception. (Psalm 51:5)
2. All are conceived sinful. (John 3:6)
3. Salvation is for all. (John 3:16)
4. Salvation comes by grace through faith. (Ephesians 2:8,9)
5. All can believe. (Mark 10:13-16)
6. A sinner, by definition, cannot believe. (Romans 7:14-25)

7. Only the Spirit grants faith. (1 Corinthians 2:14)
8. The saint, by definition, cannot not believe. (Romans 6:15–7:6)
9. Baptism is not an act of humans that pleases God but an act of God that washes humans. (Titus 3:5)
10. Our daily experience not only points to the ability of infants to believe but also points to a "pure" faith in infants compared to the jaded doubts of adults.

The result is that children, even infants, even the unborn, are loved by God, can believe, and are made saints by God. Baptism is for them.

Still there is this tricky question: If we are saved through faith and since faith is a gift of the Holy Spirit, should we be asking if the candidate believes *before* the baptism that gives faith? On the other hand, Baptism does not "work" if the person does not believe. So then we should ask if they believe *before* the act of Baptism, right? But then why baptize at all? The answer is beyond us, and rightfully so. These are the things of God. But he has not left our skulls empty. We can search Scripture and use our God-given reason to explain the mysteries of God as much as we can and are allowed to. We allow God to be God but do not shirk our responsibilities to read, think, and ponder.

Francis Pieper provides an explanation for this mystery and why it is still good that we ask the question, "Do you believe?"[9] The Word of God is present and active in Baptism. This Word is the tool of the Holy Spirit to create

---

[9]Francis Pieper, *Christian Dogmatics*, Vol. 3 (St. Louis: Concordia Publishing House, 1953), pp. 286,287.

faith in dead hearts. When exactly does this happen? We, as mere mortals, cannot always pinpoint the moment, and that is just fine. We only go by God's promise-Word. In the baptismal rite, we simply put this beautiful and mysterious action of the Spirit and God's creative Word into slow motion for our feeble minds. It all happens so quickly from our perspective. It is God's work after all. So we slow it down to see each frame of this motion picture: "What is your name? What do you seek? Depart, unclean spirit, make room for the Holy Spirit. Do you renounce? Do you believe? I baptize you." This last phrase ("I baptize") is pure gospel. We might think that it is not, that it is only a part of a rite. Wouldn't it be better to recite John 3:16? But the word *baptize* simply means "wash." I wash you. It is pure gospel.

Doesn't it seem strange, however, that God would ask a child to do something he or she cannot accomplish? Yes, it does. And God does this all the time. It is sort of the whole point. He says, "Be perfect, therefore, as your heavenly Father is perfect" (Matthew 5:48), knowing full well that this is an impossible task. He also told a paralytic to "Get up, take your mat" (Mark 2:11). He even told Lazarus, "Come out!" of the grave (John 11:43). When God commands, he provides in Christ. The command is at once just that, a command, and a gracious fulfillment. When Jesus told Thomas, "Stop doubting and believe" (John 20:27), he gave Thomas the faith to fulfill the command. His Word has creative power. "Let there be light" and there was light. "Believe!" and there is faith.

*Pastor: [Name], I baptize you in the name of the Father and of the Son and of the Holy Spirit. Amen.*

Now to the actual Baptism. So simple after all of that theology. Isn't this how God works? You can study a lifetime of theology, but it all comes down to Christ dying for you. The philosopher can spend a lifetime on the words "God is love" and yet it is enough for the child. Such is God, so accessible in his incarnational ways and yet so mysterious to us.

*Pastor: Let us pray.*

*Almighty and merciful God and Father, we thank and praise you that you graciously preserve and enlarge your family and have granted [Name] the new birth in Holy Baptism and made him/her a member of your Son, our Lord Jesus Christ, and an heir of his heavenly kingdom. We humbly implore you that, as he/ she now becomes your child, you would keep him/ her in his/her baptismal grace according to all your good pleasure that he/she may faithfully grow to lead a godly life to the praise and honor of your holy name and finally with all your saints obtain the promised inheritance in heaven; through Jesus Christ, your Son, our Lord, who lives and reigns with you and the Holy Spirit, one God, now and forever. Amen.*

*Pastor: Let us bless the Lord.*
*Congregation: Thanks be to God.*

*Pastor: The almighty and merciful God, the Father and + the Son and the Holy Spirit, bless and defend you. Amen.*

The final prayer and blessing sum up the baptismal rite succinctly but fully. The themes of family and inheritance, rebirth and initiation, grace and vocation, and thanksgiving and comfort are all present in this prayer that sums up this simple yet profound act of God. The baptized soul is now sent out into the world, the same crazy world Jesus sent his apostles into after he ascended into heaven. The baptized are once again marked with blessing. The triune God is on their side. The same God who sent the apostles. The same ascension promises. The same protection. The same mission. And the same outcome. Bless the Lord? Yes. Thanks be to God!